# *BARBRA*

# An Actress Who Sings

# Volume II

By
James Kimbrell
Edited by
Cheri Kimbrell

BRANDEN PUBLISHING COMPANY
BOSTON

**Library of Congress Cataloging-in-Publication Data**
(Revised for volume 2)

Kimbrell, James, 1955-1989
    Barbra, an actress who sings.

    Vol. 2 edited by Cheri Kimbrell.
    Includes bibliographical references and indexes.
    1. Streisand, Barbra.
    2. Singers--United States--Biography.
    3. Motion picture actors and actresses--United States--
      Biography.
    I. Kimbrell, Cheri.
    II. Title: Barbra.
ML420.S915K5  1989    784.5'0092'4 [B]   89-30295
ISBN 0-8283-1923-5 (v. 1)
ISBN 0-8283-1946-4 (v. 2)

**BRANDEN PUBLISHING COMPANY, Inc.**
17 Station Street
Box 843 Brookline Village
Boston, MA 02147

Young Barbra: Sober, passionate, talented,
and sure of her talents and goals.

*In Memory*
of
JAMES KIMBRELL

# CONTENTS

# PREFACE

As this book is going to press, Barbra Streisand is about to release her new film which she produced, directed and starred in, *The Prince of Tides*. The movie, based on Pat Conroy's book, is scheduled for release during the Christmas 1991 season. It is the second film which Streisand has directed since her 1983 *Yentl*.

In her new movie, co-star Nick Nolte delivers what critics are describing as Nolte's best work to date. Streisand, the director, has brought out an unprecedented performance in Nolte. Her 24-year-old son, by actor Elliott Gould, makes his film debut in the role of her son.

Streisand sings the soundtrack for *The Prince of Tides*--the first time she has sung a song in over two years. In a September 1991 interview, Streisand told *Vanity Fair* that she had no idea what sound would come out her mouth.

Barbra has a new romantic interest in composer James Newton Howard, who wrote the music for the soundtrack. She was introduced to him by her close friends Marilyn and Alan Bergman, the oscar-winning lyricists who have written many hit tunes for Barbra including *The Way We Were*.

Streisand has also just released a four CD collection of songs which she has privately recorded over the last thirty years. This retrospective set is a collection of rare and never before released songs titled, *Just for the Record*. Some of the recordings date back to when the singer was thirteen years old.

CHERI KIMBRELL

# FOREWORD

May 1991

Galveston, Texas

Dear James,

Although you will not in a million years receive this letter, I had to attempt this impossible and futile feat--not for me, of course, as you and I are in continuous communication. How ludicrous to write a letter to a dead person! Yet what better way to explain to your readers what happened to you between Volume I and Volume II of Barbra Streisand's biography.

After ten years of diligent interviewing, writing, re-writing, editing and spending large sums of your income and most of your free time on this project, at long last, you finished one of your most ambitious works. You managed to capture the life and work of one of the world's greatest, most misunderstood stars ever--one who has artfully maintained her position at the top of the top for over 25 years, a quarter of a century. *Barbra* was my gift to you back in 1976, when "I turned you onto to her", as we said back then. And now *Barbra* is your final gift to the world.

We all tried to dissuade you; it's true. We thought you were wasting your poetic talents, to be spent elsewhere , on more "classic" material. But the genre of biography as an art form turned out to be one of your *forte*, as your heart-warming *Sippi* biography proved when you chronicled the life of our bittersweet Southern grandma.

So, you were right in the end. But what an ironic and tragically cruel twist of fate that you should have to lose your life just as your first published book was about to go to press and be released into the world!

It somehow fell upon me to see that the first volume of *Barbra* be promoted in the media. There were so few voices left to speak for you, since you were no longer able to speak for yourself... How sad that you were deprived of your joy of promoting your master-work. Your long-awaited dream was finally here and you weren't able to enjoy the fruits of your labor. Such tragedy--in the classic tradition!

On the plane to Boston to meet with your publisher, I felt a dull sense of "what am I doing on this plane? This is Jim's book--he should be flying to the East Coast to promote his big book, not me!" It only deepened the wound.

So, after three trips to Boston to work with your publisher in promoting *Barbra--An Actress Who Sings* (Volume I), I also had the privilege to edit the remaining manuscript now appearing as Volume II.

It was a herculean task in hammering away, day after day, on that computer, trying to sort out all the maze of all these chapters, over six weeks, eight hours a day. I am not ashamed to admit that many times I cried and sobbed in the publisher's office, especially on hitting upon a particularly brilliant observation or situations familiar to me. There were also moments when I chided you--in silence, of course--for grammar or punctuation errors, or being vague with a sentence--just as we used to when we were teenagers. Then we thought every book perfect; now, I know better. However, I will do my best in making yours a perfect one.

I remember so vividly those nights we stayed up till dawn as high school students, drinking hot tea, discussing great literature and trying our hands at poetry and essay writing. We gently but honestly critiqued each other's work: you were my mentor all along, and I was your ardent pupil.

So how ironic that I should end up being your final editor--me, of all people, your *student*; but then, how fitting. After all, you taught me everything I know about literature and language. You'll note some major linguistic differences between the two volumes. I did a "Hemingway meat-and-potato job" on Volume II, although my personal preference leans toward D. H. Lawrence. So, surprisingly ironic that you *lawrenced* up your book, when you so clearly advocated the sparse, simple "fifty cent words" of a Hemingway over the three dollar words of a poetic Lawrence that I originally preferred.

But, Jim, not for a *biography*! Here's where we would have launched into a major battle. Oh, how we argued! I could almost hear you protesting vehemently behind my computer terminal seat over many of the changes from a fancy word to a simple one.

I wanted to increase readership--expand the big dream even bigger--even if it meant throwing away the thesaurus of which you were so fond.

So, Jim, here it is: Volume II published posthumously, just as Volume I was. In fact, you died just as the first big review appeared in *Kirkus Reviews*. On the day your publisher called you to tell you the good news, you had died. Instead, I had to live to see to it that your big dream was accomplished. It is one of my finer achievements, I assure you.

I am your Jeannie Greene; you're my Youngblood Hawke (Herman Wouk's prototype for us). What finer sentiment than that?

We were a strange, psychically-bound team--I felt I lost a major internal root when you died. How alike we were, really! So much of me went to that grave with you--no one can ever know. How much I truly adored you, James, will have to remain unspoken--perhaps this final tribute, gesture of love and respect, will remain as the last tangible memento of my highest regard for you. Your great wit, of which I have not seen equalled in my lifetime, of your keen, sharp intelligence and knowledge, of your vast talents and abilities, and of your unfathomable athletic prowess, fascinating personality, and remarkable unmatched sense of humor. But most, for your unfailing kindness and human empathy.

If ever I were ever to write one of those *Reader's Digest* "My Most Memorable Character", by far mine would be **James Kimbrell**!

I procrastinated a good three months before completing this brief Foreword, knowing somehow that it must get done.

## 14--James Kimbrell

It stirred up emotions that I had long since buried, in order to merely *survive*. I, somehow, knew that this little letter to my dead brother was going to leave me a crumpled mass of tears and pain, agony and remembrances of what a great loss I have suffered at the hands of fate--what a great loss to the world when you, my brother, James Daniel Kimbrell, died at the early age of thirty-four--February 8, 1989.

Goodbye, Jim. Better still: *au revoir!*

Your loving sister,

Cheryl Anne Kimbrell

# Chapter 1

## "Slapstick Streisand"

Before the new and hot director Peter Bogdanovich's acclaimed drama *The Last Picture Show* was released, superagent Sue Mengers found her client another directing job, a picture already committed to two other actor clients, the project which started out as one movie (*A Glimpse of Tiger* for Elliott Gould) and became *What's Up, Doc?* for Barbra Streisand and Ryan O'Neal. Early in 1971 Gould had abandoned the filming of the production which was, ironically, turned into the highly successful Streisand vehicle.

The industry was amazed when the actress assumed the *Glimpse of Tiger* role from her alienated husband. After having filmed for little more than one week in New York, the Elliott Gould picture closed down after some well-publicized battles: *Gould vs. the producer Jack Brodsky; Gould vs. director Anthony Harvey*; and even *Gould vs. co-star Kim Darby*. The actual script must have been a very compelling story to induce not only Elliott Gould to buy the property but for Streisand subsequently to agree to star in the comedy (with a sex-change rewrite in the featured role).

Director Harvey, celebrated for *The Lion in Winter*, described the picture as a typically American story, "a Woodstock with a plot." Manhattan filming began in late February 1971 after two weeks' rehearsal, months before *What's Up Doc?* would begin shooting in San Francisco. On the first day, director Harvey demanded that two of Gould's visitors leave the set, actors David Carradine and Barbara Hershey, and Gould was so angry he fired him. Accused of tantrums and no-shows, Gould was merely convinced that the director would have to be fired but has acknowledged a physical confrontation with Darby.

The actor was so enraged that his co-producer Jack Brodsky reinstated the director the next day that bodyguards were deemed necessary to protect the others. The studio declared the actor a victim of "emotional and physical exhaustion" after six back-to-back films. An actor unable to decline a role, Gould had appeared in five films in a year and a half, at a time when his estranged wife was relaxing her professional burdens. No one knew, or was telling, of the actor's reasons for the withdrawal, but many rumors were flourishing about his wild existence as a crazy religious hippie freak.

When *Tiger* imploded, it was difficult to figure fact from furor, such claims as that Streisand accepted the re-shooting to preclude a complicated lawsuit with her separated husband, but actually Gould was found financially responsible and spent years repaying the aborted production expenses. It was only a few weeks later that the Streisand version of *A Glimpse of Tiger* was announced in April 1971, the new star signed for the Warners property. The film commitment evolved into the promising comedy *What's Up, Doc?*, produced and directed by Peter Bogdanovich. The Bogdanovich/Streisand/O'Neal team (another convenient Sue Mengers package deal) abandoned the *Tiger* picture and chose a completely separate vehicle.

Streisand's professional life had been so demanding and painful that after her fourth film, *The Owl and the Pussycat*, she had not worked for over eighteen months, on the verge of seriously considering retirement, she thought, not even reading screenplays. Having waited more than a year-and-a-half for this fifth film, a dozen "confirmed" projects would also be announced for the actress in this year. In selecting Bogdanovich as her director before his name-making film *The Last Picture Show* was released, Streisand was once again ahead of the time. She instantly chose the film-maker based on his black-and-white drama which she viewed as a rough cut in early May 1971, after the first reel urging the chief Warner Brothers mogul, John Calley, "I want him," as she later told the director. In tears by the poignant picture, she hoped that Bogdanovich would direct her dramatic breakthrough.

Bogdanovich disliked the *Glimpse of Tiger* screenplay by Herman Raucher (*Summer of '42*), complaining to Calley and Streisand, who were chagrined that he disliked their project. "This script they had was a kind of a comedy-drama with a lot of social overtones, and I didn't like it at all." [6-72 *Films & Filming*] Streisand must have appreciated the story, as had her husband, and she probably would have preferred the *Tiger* project to the replacement. Bogdanovich prevailed in his wishes to film a screwy comedy, asking for a kind of remake of the 1938 *Bringing Up Baby* classic. Finally, the actress was convinced by her agent to accept the change.

Having been commissioned for the project, the director quickly made it his own, as though he had been saving ideas for years to apply to a comedy. *A Glimpse of Tiger* would have been a serious picture, but Bogdanovich sketched an outline with a wacky but endearing premise to John Calley. The director was eager to do a Streisand picture, winning the mogul's acceptance with a three-sentence proposal which had only then occurred to him: "Let's do a screwball comedy. Barbra will play a wacky girl and Ryan will be a musicologist who gets involved with her. It will be a farce." Calley was intrigued by the director, who envisioned Streisand as a seventies Carole Lombard. The co-star would be the *Love Story* actor, Ryan O'Neal, whom Streisand had dated throughout 1971, the California Golden Boy appropriate for the seemingly younger and younger Barbra Streisand.

Signed to the project, but with the actors' upcoming commitments elsewhere limiting their availability, Bogdanovich had only the months from May to August in which to prepare for a brand-new production. The producer/ director huddled with *Bonnie and Clyde* screenwriters Robert Newman and David Benton for four days while the writers expanded his original concept, taking two weeks afterwards to complete the first draft, which was judged inadequate, as was their next version. After the second attempt, Streisand was uncertain about the writing, as was Bogdanovich, who desperately requested that Buck Henry revise the script, as the actress apparently suggested. The director was frantic lest both actors cancel, and Calley committed *The Owl and the Pussycat* scripter Buck Henry as one of the collaborators.

Having been requested to better the woman's role, Henry panicked at the six-week deadline but managed to revise the screenplay to the complete satisfaction of most. All four writers conferred on the revisions, delivering an acceptable screenplay in two weeks, although they continued to enhance their work in the last days. Streisand had been offended by John Simon's physical obsession with her *Owl and the Pussycat* appearance, and she may have influenced the parody of the critic in this film.

Buck Henry admittedly obscured Judy's role, unintentionally, by embellishing the other elements of the script, especially noticeable to both the leading actor and actress when the talented supporting players threatened to steal the picture at the director's mandatory read-through. Chagrined about the unusual preparation, the star protested to the director, "Are you giving me line readings?" Although many film directors do not rehearse at all, Bogdanovich laboriously practiced scenes with the actors in early July for at least two weeks and enacted the performances himself, as the actors should repeat, which initially bothered the actress until she realized the benefit.

Co-star Madeline Kahn was admittedly too awed by Streisand to attempt any ego competition, and she had balked at signing because she was so afraid of the superstar, especially in her own film debut. Her agent convinced her to sign, and the director calmed her fears that her own footage might be cut, anxiety stemming from the false rumors about Anne Francis and *Funny Girl*. "I was a little apprehensive about Barbra. I had heard that a lot of performers wound up on the cutting-room floor in her movies, but I figured we're both Jewish, we're both from New York, I sing and she sings-- so why be scared? And Peter had control." [7-73 *After Dark*]

"It was a movie about three people and there's only so much you could cut out of it and still have the movie make sense. So I took a chance and it turned out fine. I really liked her and we had some good talks and I thought we could really be friends, but she has so many pressures, and she's unavailable a lot on the set, and we never became close or anything. I got a glimpse of what it's like to be a really big superstar. I don't think I'd like that." [Rex Reed's 1977 *Valentines & Vitriol*]

The cast planned to begin rehearsing July 15 with the filming scheduled to begin two weeks later in either San Francisco or New York City, or even Chicago, although script complications threatened more delays. The screenplay was still incomplete three weeks before cameras were to roll, so the start-date was advanced one month. Signed to the picture was cinematographer Laszlo Kovacs, who would also shoot the *For Pete's Sake* comedy two years later.

Although *What's Up, Doc?* was to be a contemporary comedy with music, including a handful of songs, Streisand was sold on the Bogdanovich project that no musical production numbers were intended, nor would any singing to pre-recorded songs be required. The actress agreed to sing "As Time Goes By" live, in a parody of Humphrey Bogart. With the *What's*

*Up, Doc?* budget at only $4.6 million, and the grosses over thirty million, Streisand profited more from this comedy than from her previous movies, receiving not only her customary salary but a percentage of the net profits-- although the uncertain actress gambled and sold her box office points back to the studio for an additional $2.5 million in upfront cash.

Bogdanovich: "Titles can upset people. I remember Barbra Streisand thinking, `Oh, no, no. I'm not going to be in a picture called *What's Up, Doc?*' [7-73 Interview]

"Barbra really didn't want to do the picture at all, but she signed a contract which, miraculously, gave her no script approval. The reason she signed that contract was because her agent was also my agent. And Ryan O'Neal's agent." [Judith Crist's *Take 22 - Moviemakers on Moviemaking*]

He had to pacify the actress about the script, assuring her of its promise and insisting that if she would trust him, he could ensure she would still be the focus of the comedy. Although the humor pivoted on O'Neal as the straight man, in the end Streisand managed to hold the crazed elements together as the uniquely unifying force.

The director also noted of the actress, "She was another one who was dragged kicking and screaming through the picture. She thought we were going to do something else, and I suppose I tricked her. She'd make trouble occasionally about things that she didn't think were funny, and I'd just laugh at her. She'd ask me what I was laughing at and I'd tell her she was cute. She wouldn't know what to say to that." [Jon Tuska's *The Contemporary Director*]

Bogdanovich called *What's Up, Doc?* "a madcap comedy with absolutely no socially redeeming features at all," their G-rated family concept in contrast to all the bleak, violent, sexually explicit R-rated films of the day. "It's an unpretentious but expensive picture." [11-21-71 *L.A. Times*] The director constructed an homage to American comedy, an old-fashioned slip-on-the-banana-skin type of farce. Although comedy is as old as the stage, slapstick was the specialty of film art, traced to the earliest days of Hollywood when vaudeville became immortalized on celluloid. Howard Hawkes' 1938 screwball comedy *Bringing Up Baby* was the role model for the 1972 Streisand-O'Neal tale. Cary Grant had played a paleontologist and Katharine Hepburn a millionaire lawyer's daughter, the characters in mad pursuit of a leopard, a dinosaur bone and a dog. Before filming, Bogdanovich sent O'Neal to meet with Cary Grant, who told him not to be too comical but to play it straight, and the veteran Howard Hawkes said to the young director, "Don't let them be cute."

*What's Up, Doc?* varied the *Bringing Up Baby* theme: four identical tartan overnight bags from four dissimilar characters are hopelessly confused at a San Francisco hotel: a government spy's secret papers; a wealthy matron's jewels; a scientist's prehistorical bones; the daffy Judy's change of clothing, basically her unmentionables. Certain unsavory characters covet the various belongings, and with everyone wanting everyone else's travelling cases in the first place, the mad confusion and the resulting wild pursuit between the owners and thieves of the various valises are luxuriously hilarious, and utterly unable to follow. A cross-cutting cinematic technique developed the cheerfully absurd plot, such as it was....

Bogdanovich was interviewed for a June 1972 *What's Up, Doc?* cover story by *Film and Filming* critic Gordon Gow. The director described his new picture as "a kind of a combination of a Feydeau farce, with much running in and out of rooms and slamming of doors, and a kind of screwball comedy, such as *Bringing Up Baby* was-- the sort of comedy Hollywood made in the 1930s and the early 1940s." Other than Carole Lombard, he said only Streisand could play Judy. "It requires a star personality, but it's not a star vehicle." The director has also rationalized that he knew how celebrated a star the young actress was, but her scarcity of film credits kept his regard in proportion. He was unable to consider Barbra Streisand in the same manner he did legendary screen goddesses such as Lombard.

Streisand was in especially good spirits throughout the shooting of the light comedy. As Judy Maxwell, the actress was sexier than ever before, newly slim and with a gorgeous bronze tan. The director deliberately dressed her in a very basic wardrobe, with simple makeup and wearing long straight hair, all to underscore her comic abilities. With little or no makeup and no wigs, she had few costume changes, one outfit being only jeans. Allowing her "star" image to be ignored, she seemed more natural when photographed from all angles. The director told the actress that only he was allowed temperamental behavior while filming, and in later years he joked about handling the actress, "I simply say, 'Shut up and give me a little kiss, will ya?' or 'Stick out your boobs-- they're beautiful.' And after that she's fine-- for the next ten minutes."

Good notices would praise the actress' polished self-presence, no longer the awkward kook; ably-suited to the gamin role, her own personality was caricatured. The actress herself believed that her own instincts and intelligence interfered with the characterization, but reviewers were to relish the "typecasting" of an eccentric actress in a kooky role. Judy Maxwell's roguish and saucy charm was intermingled with eccentricity and an encyclopedic memory, a footloose free-spirit meddling in the life of a square professor.

Initially going on location in the late summer in San Francisco where half the film would be shot, the then-final airport sequence was shot first, with a transistor microphone strapped to Streisand's body under her slacks. She was said to have attempted to elude an ardent male fan by hiding in the ladies' room. When the young man followed her, Johnny Weismuller, Jr., rescued the star by going after the youth in the midst of the mystified women inside, like a scene in the movie.

Unlike the splashy production numbers her previous films had entailed, the sequence of Judy's singing an all-too-brief chorus of "As Time Goes By" was filmed high atop the city in a half-completed penthouse nightclub.  Sprawled atop the hotel piano, her face was virtually invisible behind her tumbling hair. For another crucial hotel scene (but reproduced on the set), Bogdanovich showed the actress exactly how she should cling to the ledge from her fingernails, hiding from Howard's fiancee and wearing only a towel.

Without the San Francisco setting, *What's Up Doc?* would not have been the same, mostly because of the madcap pursuit around the fabled up-and-down locale.  Cheerfully modeled on the wild Sennett comedies, the action sequence was as rapid as Peter Yates' *Bullitt* which it parodies with a touch of Hitchcock and Keaton.  The director has written that the famous chase scene was inspired by his reading of Buster Keaton's memoirs. The action footage required much of the location time to preserve on film, and after two weeks of crucial outdoor shooting in Northern California, the schedule was extended to four weeks plus, the chase sequence proving to be more complicated than anticipated.

Lasting for a big chunk of the 90-minute film, the twelve-minute footage required 19 days, 32 stunt men and $1 million to film.  Despite a permit to drive the three cars down the long flights of steps, the film-makers had to pay considerably for damages.  At the inevitable San Francisco Bay climax of the crazed scramble, a bit of humor was the proof that Volks-wagens do actually float (if for only a few minutes).  It is regrettable that the city's loveable cable cars were not somehow written into the screenplay with what would have been certainly hilarious results.

The fright-eyed expression on the faces of the stars was genuine, according to O'Neal.  Stunt persons doubled for the actors, including a man masquerading as the actress when the cart careens down the steepest street in the world, the tortuous

Lombard Street. It was necessary for the actual actors to ride in their improvised conveyance to film the close-up sequences down the other long hills, and both were terrified.

Stunt feats in action sequences have been a heated Hollywood issue of spectacle-before-safety since the three tragic 1982 deaths of *The Twilight Zone* actors. High-flying car spectacle is in demand by a glazed public, and some of Streisand's films have fed this vicarious fantasy. Veteran stunt man Ted Duncan was involved in the *What's Up, Doc?* finale and remembers being contracted in 1972 by stunt coordinator Paul Baxley to drive a limousine off the end of the San Francisco pier into the Bay.

Duncan's story is that he insisted on being given an auxiliary one-hour tank of oxygen so that in the event of an emergency in the frigid, 40-feet deep bay, he would be protected beyond the two-minutes' worth of oxygen he was expected to use. Baxley refused to delay filming, and Duncan refused to proceed with the stunt. Replacement Dick Butler was given the extra oxygen, but the impact of the water collapsed the roof, and it took him five minutes to struggle free, his panicked ascent so rapid he broke an eardrum. Stunt director Baxley would later insist that no such accident befell the man and that the scene was within the margin of safety. "Duncan called me at midnight the night before to say an ear specialist had told him he shouldn't do the stunt. What he really needed was a heart specialist." [2-7-83 *L.A. Times*] The cavalier attitude toward fear and the discrepancy concerning who suffered the eardrum problem should be noted.

O'Neal was hurt during the filming, according to society reports noting that the actor had tripped over Streisand's heavy fake ermine coat, which she had dropped. Later, the seeming sprained muscle proved to be a problem spinal disc ruptured by the accident, which necessitated surgery. The woman marveled at his bravery, "I never heard him complain. I never dreamed he was hurt that badly."

O'Neal told reporters that his co-star's insecure acting technique was to accept the situation as being the worst it could be and then everything could only be improved. The perfectionist director with the perfectionist performer shot endless retakes, but the actor noted that when she insisted that she could do a tenth or eleventh take better than the previous eight or nine, she would eventually yield to Bogdanovich who would be convinced that the scene was perfect as it was. Of her multi-layered characterization, O'Neal said: "She felt that Judy was sort of a fantasy, and if you're playing a fantasy you can go many different ways because a fantasy can do anything." With the actress continuing to be late for the daily shooting, a location event was scheduled for a mandatory 8:00 a.m. beginning in order to conclude by 11:00, when the site would no longer be available. Although the actress forced herself to be punctual, technical complications ironically delayed the shooting. [4-72 *Show*]

Streisand stayed at the Nob Hill Huntington Hotel, where she was rumored to have received a call from a newsman impostor asking for her reaction to the supposed automobile accident death of her *On a Clear Day You Can See Forever* co-star Yves Montand and wife Simone Signoret. An unknown crank caller continually telephoned the hotel as well, finally reaching the star's suite when he said the call concerned "her son," who had flown with his maternal grandmother to San Francisco for one weekend. Jason's nurse intercepted the phone call of the anonymous male caller threatening to abduct the boy unless he could meet the actress and express his love.

The dangerously unbalanced caller promised to give the six-year-old boy "a good home." Streisand was distraught, but O'Neal increased security, routed calls to his suite and spent as much time possible in Jason's presence. Streisand apparently sent the boy to his father after the kidnap scare, which affected her concentration the next day when filming on location at Fisherman's Wharf.

After little more than a month of filming in San Francisco, the company returned to Burbank where the sets had been constructed for the hotel interiors. She requested that the set be closed when she agreed to the nude bathtub scene (the sudsy bubbles obscuring any real nudity). She was very frustrated by a Los Angeles society writer who proclaimed, "Barbra Streisand stormed off the set because she didn't like the color of a bathtub," when in reality the scene had to be delayed until a bathtub was built tall enough to hide her breasts. She had been baffled that the television reporter could lie before all the world about a totally fabricated incident. In the collaborative film industry, Streisand knew that an enduring success for an actress would be impossible with that kind of unprofessional behavior.

During a television interview, O'Neal defended his co-star: "Everyone knocks her for being hard to please, but if she were treated like the movie queen she is, then she wouldn't have room to complain and she would feel more at ease." In turn, the actress would recollect, "Ryan was probably the easiest actor I've ever had to work with, and the most fun. Just terrific."

Dan Knapp was one journalist who sought either to substantiate or dispel the mythical bitch-goddess Barbra Streisand image in two interviews. The reporter had been overwhelmed by the star's huge, opulent dressing room, but she had immediately complained herself. "Isn't it awful? I didn't ask for it and it makes me feel uncomfortable. It's not good for morale on the set." She was embarrassed by the stained glass windows, crystal chandeliers and Victorian furniture. Dining with his co-star, O'Neal interpreted a no-win position of complaining and being considered difficult-- or accepting the luxury and seeming to flaunt her stardom.

The actor had already been involved with Streisand for nearly a year, and their intimate and playful lunch was witnessed, with the superstar plainly deferring to the less-famous male, wanting her boyfriend to be the focus of the interview.

The inevitable nasty rumors had accused O'Neal of using Streisand to further his career. Dan Knapp left with a knowledge that this was a superstar obviously maligned by a vindictive press, and her sincerity was confirmed at a follow-up meeting in the spring of 1972 in her home. The O'Neal romance had ended, but their comedy was a smash hit and the actors remained good friends. Streisand's oft-quoted complaint: "I wish that, just once, someone would write about the real me. I'm really not what they say I am. Sometimes I'd like to be, though. That other bitchy person, I mean. My god, I'd be so much more interesting."

The director Peter Bogdanovich has always denied any problems working with his star, her perfectionism being no problem for him. He remembered that when the actress resisted him, he would remind her that she had wanted strong direction, although he could recall no serious quarrels. "I don't think there ever was a Barbra 'The Terrible.'" He found her very easy-going, brimming with suggestions and self-doubt which prompted the numerous questions about her own performance, behavior which he believed was quite normal and actually beneficial. "Barbra is difficult only in delightful way. After all, she's a woman. I only wish there were more women like her in the industry." [3-12-72 *L.A. Times*] The director felt Streisand was so much an excellent, confident and cooperative actress that she did not really require direction. Some years later, he described her as hard to please, frequently finding something wrong or some area of complaint, but he said he pacified her by being pleasant and full of praise.

During one interview together, the star sat in her director's lap and fed him pumpkin ice cream, describing Bogdanovich as "a horny bastard but brilliant." She added, "An opinionated and autocratic director. He knows how he wants to do things and doesn't waste a lot of time. Even if he's wrong, it's the right way to do it. I gave up script approval, costume approval, everything to him." Peter Bogdanovich's wife, Polly Platt, was estranged from her husband but designed the sets and costumes. [11-14-71 *N.Y. Times*] Streisand later remembered relinquishing script approval as she so earnestly wished to work with the director. "That was a technical mistake. All through that movie I was just trying not to show my hostility toward the material. It was trying to be like *Bringing Up Baby*, but it wasn't. That was a brilliant film." *Up the Sandbox* [press conference]

# Chapter 2

"Remember Screwball Comedies?"

A Warner Bros. studio press release: "She isn't always a hit with her studio bosses because she is a highly individualized person with an abundance of talent, a drive that won't stop and enough eccentricities to make her bizarre but not grotesque." Such candid but loveable confessions indicate why Barbra Streisand may still be associated with the studio for whom she has made her three most successful films.

The sixteen weeks' shooting of *What's Up, Doc?* included a December 12, 1971 rematch of the actors, although filming had officially ended in October. Negative advance preview reception to the last scene meant that the film-makers added another. The original bittersweet ending in which Judy and Howard part at the airport was altered so that instead they confess their love on the airplane, the upbeat finale shot in TWA's ubiquitous mockup airliner thought to be more commercial.

The *Love Story* dig was a harmless bit of humor which most critics enjoyed, especially laughing at a picture they themselves had knocked. Some reviewers admonished fans not to laugh too much at Streisand's winking reference ("Love means never having to say you're sorry") lest they miss O'Neal's blistering reply ("That's the dumbest thing I ever heard"). The "in" joke laughed at the famous line from the actor's star-making movie, but some critics hailed Streisand's cheerful statement as deliberately provocative. She bats her eyes followed by a wide-open expression bespeaking innocence; critics accepted the coy look as a broad indication to any uncertain moviegoer that this is all good-natured fun and to reveal to her peers that none of this was her idea...

It is disappointing that no soundtrack album was released from this film comedy. If soundtracks were feasible for *The Owl and the Pussycat* (mostly dialogue) and for *The Way We Were* (mostly instrumental), then surely the three tunes Streisand sang in the *What's Up, Doc?* smash would have warranted a recording. Reportedly the star herself declined the proposed soundtrack, full-length versions of the songs she sang in the film, plus comic dialogue as had been done for *Pussycat*. Trying to grow beyond *What's Up, Doc?*, the actress decided to focus on her serious film, *Up the Sandbox*.

The comedy's onscreen singing excluded production numbers, but in a studio session the actress-singer performs Cole Porter's "You're the Top" while a woman's hand was shown turning scrapbook pages of the credits. Overwhelmingly titillating the audience later in the movie, the performer delivers a brief Bogart impersonation and sings "As Time Goes By" atop the piano of the hotel penthouse, the song recorded live at the San Francisco Hilton. Streisand persuaded her co-star to accompany her on the light duet at the film's closing title sequences, reprising "You're the Top." In the last few seconds O'Neal banters with the star about her nose. "Watch it," she warns.

Determined not to spoil the comedy by revealing too many of the gags, the director used behind-the-scenes documentary footage for the film's trailer. Concluding that the critics needed a real-life audience to appreciate the laughter, not being surrounded merely by fellow reviewers, a semi-successful plan was Bogdanovich's last-minute decision to include the public at the press screening. The advance preview was held only days before the Radio City opening, but unfortunately, the public-- unhappy at being restricted-- managed to stampede the reserved seating section and important critics were left without seats. The entire event was troubling to the public and press alike and was thought to have affected some of the reviews.

When Streisand's and O'Neal's ardor for each other cooled, the actor returned to his wife in a well-publicized but short-lived reconciliation. He escorted Leigh Taylor-Young, with whom he was soon to divorce, to an advance Sunday night showing of *What's Up, Doc?* at Grauman's Chinese Theater. Streisand did not attend the preview because, at least in part, her next production *Up the Sandbox* required her to be filming early in the morning.

With *What's Up, Doc?* costing only $4 million, the box office potential of the brisk 94-minute comedy was great; the then-rare "G" rating was especially promising in an era of socially weighty pictures. Critic Winfred Blevins astutely observed, "If we can't remember what was so funny five minutes after we leave the theater, that is the point." Crowds flocked to see the bright comedy from two of the most desired stars in Hollywood, their romance and all the attendant rumors only boosting the box office. Ads pointedly exclaimed: "The girl from *Funny Girl* meets the boy from *Love Story...*" Some commentators who took the title too seriously compared the carrot-munching Judy Maxwell to Bugs Bunny and the befuddled Howard Bannister to Elmer Fudd. When a film sequel was tentatively planned, the title was a play upon the original: *That All, Folks!*

The film's success earned Barbra Streisand *Box Office* magazine's "Box Office Champ of the Year" for 1972, the actress' first such designation. *What's Up, Doc?* is still Streisand's second most successful picture, behind only *A Star Is Born*. The domestic receipts rivaled, even exceeded, *Funny Girl's* smash profits, especially with the one-third-less production costs.

Bogdanovich later recalled, "What's Up, Doc? was fun to make almost all the way through. Streisand was really wonderful with me, and I really enjoyed working with her. I like her a lot. She's a cute girl, but she wasn't a movie star to me, certainly not a superstar. She was just a nice, interesting girl." The director noted that her initial animosity toward the project was lessened when she made more money from *Doc* than from any film until *A Star Is Born*, although the three million she earned could have been doubled had she not lacked faith in the comedy. [Jon Tuska's *The Contemporary Director*]

"On Doc she told John Calley, the head of the studio: `I'll bet you ten grand it doesn't gross $5 million.' Calley said he didn't take the bet only because he knew Barbra wouldn't pay him. The picture will make $35 million [actual receipts being $50 million], and Barbra sold her piece of the picture back to the studio for $2.5 million." Streisand later called Bogdanovich to clarify what the glowing personal reviews meant by her "charming and likeable performance", which he interpreted as an actress' being natural and free of the period trappings of her musicals. He candidly noted that when she then made the drama she so earnestly wanted, *Up the Sandbox* was a commercial failure. [Judith Crist's *Take 22 - Moviemakers on Moviemaking*]

Bogdanovich eventually dragged Streisand to the Chinese Theater where they sat upstairs, the star impressed by the audience's riotous laughter to a comedy she thought not refined enough for her. By the end of filming, with Streisand and O'Neal no longer an item in the nation's gossip columns, Peter Bogdanovich had begun his modest romance with the actress. Almost like a scene in their comedy, he escorted her to the Director's Guild awards at the Beverly Hilton and had to hold his napkin to her face so that they could talk in peace without the paparazzi interference. They were dating friends in 1972, he evidently unfazed by her disdain for their film.

At the *Up the Sandbox* press luncheon, she vehemently complained, "I detested Doc... I didn't grow.... It did nothing for me." She felt able to be frank about her dislike because the comedy had been released for over a year already. She appreciated that the public was pleased and made happier but hoped they would enjoy *Up the Sandbox* also. The actress was the film's harshest critic, candidly criticizing the comedy for years. The humor did not seem very funny to her, especially when she compared it to *Funny Girl*. "I hated it with a passion. What interests me is how so many people liked it. I was embarrassed to do that film. I thought it was infantile humor and not one-sixteenth of the film that it was trying to emulate." [Joseph Gelmis interview/late 1972 *Newsday*]

She told another reporter, "I felt used." When she was promoting her next and sixth film *Up the Sandbox* in two December 1972 press conferences, she reiterated about *What's Up, Doc?* "I didn't enjoy making it. I thought it was a silly piece of material. I thought I would be dealing in something very personal, interesting and important. And what was it? A puff of smoke, a piece of fluff. Now, there's room for both things, you know, but I didn't feel I was growing as an artist.

"It was a technical error on my part. I gave up script approval, and I made a mistake. I saw *The Last Picture Show*, and I gave him [Bogdanovich] script control. The script was ready the day before we started shooting. I hadn't worked for 19 months before that, and then I had to try not to show my real feelings, my hostility, while we were shooting. The picture was trying to be 1940's. It's not, but it was trying. I just felt it wasn't good enough." Streisand realized how candid she was being-- why she seldom consented to interviews because she hurt herself being so frank-- and she knew her colleagues would not be pleased.

When a writer prompted her that a "no comment" comment might have been sufficient, she boldly tried the truth once again, "No comment! That means it stinks, doesn't it?" Streisand's motivations in having selected *Up the Sandbox* as her next film are obvious, considering her disgruntled attitude toward her lightweight comedy. The fact that the film of her choice failed commercially seems not to bother her. She obviously feels that her tastes and the public's are quite different and she will try to honor her own vision.

If the actress disliked the comedy so much, considering it so inferior to its predecessor, *Bringing Up Baby*, it is ironic that so many critics enthusiastically applauded the film and her performance, highly flattering notices for both the director and the star. That no message was intended seemed frivolous to the self-conscious actress. In paying homage to the stylish 1930's pictures, Peter Bogdanovich intended to create an abstract comedy, a deliberately derivative screwball. The genre had long been dead, depressed after the World War II realism, killed in the 1960's by the important, socially significant comedies.

Sight and verbal gags abound in this romantic escapist picture, a riotous comedy of errors, the screwball as always crucially dependent upon a plot device of coincidence. For the deliberately whimsical *What's Up, Doc?*, it was mandatory for audiences to abandon any disbelief and enjoy oneself self-indulgently. The comedy is damned funny: how else can one explain its appeal?

Most likely most modern audiences knew nothing of the antecedents to *What's Up, Doc?*, which was categorized as a film genre of tribute by transfiguration, but in actuality, the comedy was equally comprised of originality and borrowed inspiration. The director insisted that the picture was not intended as an homage to screwball, being instead merely similar. He said *Doc* was only inspired by *Bringing Up Baby*, not a remake, the basic plot a rather routine comic device. The 30's and 40's genres blended into the earlier 20's slapstick of Laurel and Hardy, Buster Keaton, Keystone Cops, and others, the Mack Sennett pie-in-the-face kind of farce dating from the earliest tradition of Hollywood. Critics also distilled comic themes from classic Warner Bros. cartoons brought to life, including a parody of the *Bullitt* chase scene much like a "Road

Runner" cartoon sequence. What must critics have thought when, with Bogdanovich having modeled the chase scene after Peter Yates' *Bullitt*, Yates then modeled their *For Pete's Sake* production after the *What's Up, Doc?* screwball antics....

Reviewers alternately preferred or rejected the actress' taming her high-powered superstar wattage to portray the eccentric college girl in a fast-paced farce. Those who had especially resented Streisand's being the focus of the earlier pictures greeted this comedy with pleasure. Pleased that the starless actress deferred to the other characters with a perfect blending, many critics dropped their strident label to praise a subtle yet stunning performance. Streisand's interpretation was as though she had declined to imitate Katharine Hepburn, the fast-talking heroine Judy M. uniquely her own. It was noted that O'Neal was caught between two women, both of whom were aggressive and domineering. Madeline Kahn as Howard's crabby fiancée was singularly effective, mightily counter-balancing the superstars in her debut role.

Critic Barry Gross considered *What's Up, Doc?* more intriguing than *Bringing Up Baby* because Streisand had more of a fight on her hands to woo the clearly stuffy O'Neal, Katharine Hepburn merely guiding a screwy man into her lair. [Spring 75 *Journal of Ethnic Studies*] *Time* magazine's Jay Cocks complained that seeing *Doc* was "like shaking hands with a joker holding a joy buzzer: the effect is both presumptious and unpleasant."

The villain of the piece, the Hugh Simon character, was based on the obnoxious, pompous critic John Simon, and a study of a film's critical reception would be woefully inadequate without the legendary reviewer who titled his *What's Up, Doc?* review "Scylla and Charybdis: Minnelli and Streisand." The actress admitted that she read her reviews for this picture and was disturbed by the personal notices, "unbelievably hostile," certainly resenting John Simon the most.

The misogynist's hatred for Barbra Streisand is no less for Liza Minnelli; about "Charybdis" he vividly slurred the former, surely amusing himself late at night with his misdirected intellect: "In the present film, Miss Streisand looks like a cross between an aardvark and an albino rat surmounted by a platinum-coated horse bun. Though she has good eyes and a nice complexion, the rest of her is a veritable anthology of disaster areas. Her speaking voice seems to have graduated with top honors from the Brooklyn Conservatory of Yentaism, and her acting consists entirely of fishily thrusting out her lips, sounding like a cabbie bellyaching at breakneck speed, and throwing her weight around." Simon was flattered that the director based "the film's heavy," Hugh Simon, on himself, but he pronounced the Yugoslavish plagiarist to be actually Peter Bogdanovich himself... [*Reverse Angle, A Decade of American Films*]

# Chapter 3

"Ryan O'Neal Loves Barbra Streisand"

After having seen a preview of Ryan O'Neal's breakthrough film, *Love Story*, Barbra Streisand became involved with the actor whom she dated throughout much of 1971, their romance culminating in their own smash hit movie. Streisand and O'Neal had already been acquainted over a year before their mutual agent Sue Mengers arranged the package deal which resulted in their comedy success.

Because of the many actresses and models who publicly rave about the modern-day Casanova's bedroom manners, Ryan O'Neal has been widely depicted as one of Hollywood's most prolific lovers. Currently settled down with Farrah Fawcett, the sexy actor has been associated with Joan Collins, Britt Eckland, Peggy Lipton, Claudine Longet, Ursula Andress and Margaret Trudeau. Streisand was one of the man's earlier partners, a relationship which endured at least over a year, beginning well before they were filming their picture. The actor had just become estranged from his second wife, Leigh Taylor-Young, when he began visiting Barbra Streisand regularly, their romance having caught fire and the couple making not-quite-anonymous outings.

In early January 1971 while the Academy Award nominations were pending, the liaison was still generally kept discreet, O'Neal's secretiveness thought to be motivated by the fear that a scandal would affect his chances of being nominated for *Love Story*. Ryan O'Neal was Hollywood's hot new actor, and the young happy lovers were a natural target for the tabloids' titillating tales.

The couple attended a party at record mogul Robert Krasnow's home, at which a paparazzo seeking cozy pictures of the young actor and actress had been rebuffed twice; he subsequently followed their car to Santa Monica, where Streisand had been taken by the O'Neal brothers, Ryan and Kevin, to a Mama Cass concert, a singer with whom she and her escorts were acquainted. After the show they were besieged when Ryan O'Neal left to retrieve their car, Streisand pleading, "I don't want to be photographed, please!" Although most of the paparazzi begrudgingly accepted her wishes, the earlier stalker continued with a barrage of flashcube shots. Kevin O'Neal leaped into the crowd to stop the aggressive Peter Borsari who ignored their desires to be left alone, and the other O'Neal was soon to help his brother.

It was unknown whether the O'Neals had actually struck anyone, but the media complaints were groundless that Streisand was asking for it and could have simply agreed to stand for a brief picture, as if any paparazzo would take a quick shot and disappear. Hostile columnists bitched that if Streisand and her companions refused to be photographed together, then they should not have made a public appearance.

The entertaining romance became widely-publicized following the public confrontation. What Streisand undoubtedly feared did occur, highly contagious tales illicitly linking the still-married Streisand to the still-married O'Neal, the Kevin O'Neal cover easily dissolved under the intense scrutiny. When Leigh Taylor-Young legally separated from her husband, the rumors increased about the man's romance, and Streisand herself was close to divorcing Elliott Gould after several years of being amicably separated.

After the Oscar ceremony, the Streisand-O'Neal romance was more open, such as his witnessing a *Barbra Joan Streisand* recording session; their association became very public in late

June 1971 when the actor escorted her to the Chinese Theater preview of his movie *Wild Rovers*. The pair had been seriously dating and just that week Streisand had filed for a divorce from Gould.

Late in the summer, the tabloids happily chronicled the actors' romance, such as revealing that he took her to the Reseda ranch where his still-friendly first wife Joanna Moore lived with his children, Griffin and Tatum, for whom the star signed autographs. Less than a month later, O'Neal took his girlfriend home to meet his parents, and yet columnists avidly followed his simultaneous outings with other women even during the *What's Up. Doc?* production. The Streisand-O'Neal romance was unusual and must have accommodated along the way the wandering adventures of the stud actor, if not of the woman herself, such as her dalliance with Kris Kristofferson, but the O'Neal relationship was pretty well spent by the end of filming, the fling having lasted about a year. At one point the young couple (O'Neal a year older) ordered the then popular gold dog tags, with pertinent information engraved in gold, the unique jewelry airmailed from Cartier's.

Streisand appreciated his respect for her personally without being overawed by her career. They both admitted theirs was a relationship of opposites attracting each other, although she regarded him as too alike temperamentally to succeed romantically with her. She considered him the only serious romance since her husband, although they avoided talk of marriage for the time being. "We both fall in love easily. You wouldn't think so, would you? I've had one marriage that didn't work; he's had two. No one's in a rush," the woman declared. [4-72 *Photoplay*] He later said of their romance: "We were able to share a kind of shyness." He learned that her timid nature during social occasions would dissipate if she was faced with phoniness.

When *What's Up, Doc?* finished, O'Neal gave his co-star an embroidered quilt for her bedroom. During the filming he had suffered considerably with back trouble, especially when worsened by an injury on the set. He underwent surgery when they returned to Los Angeles, Streisand having to go to Vegas by herself when contractually bound to the International Hotel engagement.

Streisand was pained to be unable to join her good friend when he experienced the intricate and potentially disabling spinal surgery at St. John's Hospital in Santa Monica in December 1971. "The terrible irony is that you're with some-body so much and just when you need to be with him, you can't be," she was quoted. Each day they talked for hours on the phone, and she was also able to fly back to Los Angeles on two occasions. "Ryan was lying in bed, and you know, he has that terribly irresistible little boy quality about him. I have that terrible Brooklyn Jewish need to mother. Maybe that's why we got along so well."

By then they had been together over a year, but Leigh Taylor-Young began visiting her husband every day in the hospital. Possibly the turning point in the Streisand-O'Neal romance was this hospitalization, as the prolonged convales-cence allowed the actor's wife to return to his side, the Streisand romance was never the same, it seems. Mrs. O'Neal refused to answer questions about her husband's involvement with the other woman.

Streisand and O'Neal remained friends, and he is to date the only actor to have been paired twice with the superstar actress, O'Neal later playing the comic championship fighter Kid Natural in 1979's *The Main Event*. Although the actors enjoyed a well-publicized romance, a onetime Streisand friend Muriel Harris also claimed that the actress never really cared for Ryan O'Neal, intimating that she considered him just a sexual plaything. "Of course she never really cared for Ryan O'Neal. She always dismissed him as... well, you know." It must be considered that Harris' estrangement from the actress makes her words to biographers Zec and Fowles suspicious.

Streisand may have recognized that O'Neal was no intellectual, but he clearly made her feel her own age. She was candid in her preference for men with raw animal appeal, a decade later adding, "I don't think externals are as important as many people think. I feel very secure with men of all kinds, whatever they look like, but I think most women hesitate to pair up, permanently, with a man who's... outrageously handsome. Anyway, what's inside is what tells. I never cared for dumb dons; I want a man with brains upstairs, you know?" [6-81 *Photoplay Film Monthly*]

Asked many years later why he had not married Barbra Streisand, O'Neal answered, "Well, that's very personal, and there are many reasons, but I occasionally think about it, and I'll just say this about that--If I had to marry, I mean if I was up against the wall with a rifle at my back, Babs is the girl I'd have wanted to marry." [9-79 *Photoplay Film & TV Scene*]

# Chapter 4

"A Marriage as Good as Gould:

Mr. Barbra Streisand"

A would-be child star with a doting, long-sighted mother, Elliott Goldstein danced and modeled occasionally in his early years. From the chorus of *Irma La Douce* on Broadway, the young man's first major break came when he was cast as the leading character of the 1962 musical *I Can Get It For You Wholesale*, where he met and fell in love with the future superstar Barbra Streisand, who played a minor character named Miss Marmelstein.

At 6'3", the man is nearly a foot taller than the woman whom he recognized as "an original beauty." Through the years 1963-1969 his public identity was as the superstar's husband, "Mr. Barbra Streisand," ironically a domestic drama uncannily alike the *Funny Girl* tale unfurling nightly on Broadway, later immortalized on film when the Goulds moved to Hollywood. He especially loathed discussing his own personal failures in interviews and avoided the press whom he feared would use him for access to his wife.

While the actor's trade was still floundering alongside his wife's flourishing career, he managed to perform only in road-show versions of stage musicals, but he did star on Broadway in *Drat! the Cat!* and Jules' Feiffer's *Little Murders*, neither of which stayed open longer than a few days. By a sad coincidence, one of his *Drat! the Cat!* songs was "She Touched Me," which Streisand remade into one of her million-selling hits.

The husband's classic case of psychological insecurity must have been sorely tested by his wife's assignations with the film *Funny Girl* co-star Omar Sharif, especially after the rumors developed more substance than simple hearsay. Late in the year 1967 when Sharif took Streisand to a Hollywood discotheque for an exclusive fashion show, after which they were seen dining together, Gould explained to columnist Sheilah Graham. "My wife's fairly naive about publicity. She's a young girl who is a non-conformist. She doesn't play the game. She's had a very frustrating and difficult existence and she's worked very hard to get where she is." [12-6-67 *HWD Citizen-News*]

A well-publicized Hollywood fracas occurred in late October 1968 when the Goulds and two friends were leaving a Director's Guild screening of *Bullitt*, the actor scuffling with a 21-year-old photographer Tony Rizzo who one week later sued the couple for $200,000, alleging that he had been "wrongfully, unlawfully and violently assaulted, beat and struck." The actor had apparently only pushed the paparazzo who had wanted more pictures, although his flashcubes had exploded in Streisand's face all evening. Hiding her face, she asked him to stop, pleading, "You have enough! You have enough!"

An exasperated Gould reiterated, "Haven't you got enough yet?" Rizzo impudently answered, "Sir, if you were polite and stopped walking like everyone else, we wouldn't have to bother you now." An enraged Gould leaped at him, "I'll show you who is not polite," the actor allegedly twisting a thick silver chain holding the camera, then pushing Rizzo against a car. "I'll break your camera, you son of a bitch!" The photographer taunted him, "Watch your mouth-- there are ladies present."

Streisand missed the scuffle when she and her friend Abbe Lane fled from the commotion. In avoiding excess publicity, the Goulds of course received full-scale coverage the next morning. Rizzo claimed injury to his back, shoulders and

neck, and three years later a judge awarded a modest settlement. In June of 1971, just three weeks before their divorce,
Streisand had to testify in court for her husband's trial,
although the judge had dismissed the photographer's claim
against Streisand, who had not participated in the altercation
and who would soon be the ex-Mrs. Gould.

The actor argued that his only physical contact with Rizzo
was to move him from their path. "I never struck or hit him
in any way. I was very careful to put him down as gently as
I could." He denied that he had shoved him against a car. "I
leaned him against it. I wanted to make sure he didn't fall
down," the actor told the judge in the two-day non-jury pro-
ceedings. Gould said he had asked the paparazzo many times
to cease as his actions "upset" his wife. Although Rizzo won
$6,500 in damages for his "manhandling" charges, the judge
dismissed the claims of assault and battery and then asked the
actor for his autograph. Later in the year the actress attended
a premiere of *Willy Wonka and the Chocolate Factory* with her
son, and when the same persistent paparazzo pursued her to the
restroom, she told Jason, "Stick out your tongue at that awful
man," both mother and son giggling.

Elliott Gould's only solid successes during the active years
of his marriage were starring roles in road-show musicals. Still
married to Streisand during the *Hello, Dolly!* filming, he was
on the road with *Luv*. He succeeded finally as an actor in
controversial, original and modern films featuring the rebellious
anti-hero. Ironically, the actor's first recognition came not
until after the 1969 separation from his wife with his small but
substantial role in *The Night They Raided Minsky's*, which was
a modest hit. His role as the youthful entrepreneur, Bill
Minsky, was negotiated through Streisand's agent, David
Begelman. Then during his estranged wife's production of
*Clear Day*, Gould was filming his own major picture, *Ted &
Alice & Carol & Bob*, as Streisand worded the order of names
in the title to emphasize her husband's role. A major acting

status came after this subsequent hit picture, for which he won an Oscar nomination.

The actor was astute enough to realize it was merely coincidental that his success came after being apart from his superstar wife, that it was not true that her fame had precluded his own. His experiences being vicariously exposed to celebrity eased his own transition to stardom, so that he was not deluded into believing fame was the priority in his life. Gould gained even greater distinction in the anti-military black comedy *M*A*S*H*. A man of great industry, he completed film after film, more as an actor than a movie star.

Gould's appeal was seen as reflecting the new demand for reality, for a specifically unheroic protagonist, especially for the below-30 majority of theatergoers.

Compared to his sluggish stage career, Gould achieved film stature relatively easily. Fame purged much of the pressure between the spouses, but it was too late. Would the Goulds have stayed together had he too been a superstar all those earlier years? Perhaps their marriage would have endured longer, but the man is radically different in character, his personality far more tense. To his credit, his world was larger, at least then, Gould being far more interested in international news and current events. The actor noted many years later, "Right from the start Barbra was competitive with me as far as our careers were concerned. I tried to tell her many times that she had nothing to prove. But she insisted, `Yes, there was.'" He has proclaimed their undeniable mutual love, but they were forced to divorce when "certain predestined situations neither of us could deal with without destroying one another" inevitably separated them.

Before the official announcement, rumors about an upcoming divorce had plagued the couple since mid-summer 1968, although they continued to deny any rift. A January 1969 column from Earl Wilson stated: "Barbra Streisand and her husband are having marriage problems. The problems are personal and neither will discuss them. But they're further apart now than the mere mileage that separates them." At that time neither of the Goulds issued a contradiction. An earlier column item in March 1968 had foreshadowed the separation nearly a year hence when Wilson described their altered plans to part temporarily: "It was to have been one of the friendliest trial separations on record, and finally it got so friendly they called it off."

Their first publicized alienation occurred on February 12, 1969, each mutually agreeing to part. The brief announcement from Streisand's publicist: "Barbra Streisand and her husband, Elliott Gould, have agreed to a trial separation. In a joint statement Mr. and Mrs. Gould said, `We are separating in an effort to save our marriage and not to destroy it.'" That the couple did not divorce for 2½ years proves their optimism and indicates how seriously they attempted to salvage their union. At the studio for *On a Clear Day*, the woman was besieged by press, but she would only disclose that she regretted any pain caused her fans, hoping something positive would result.

Hollywood was surprised that the actress issued that private of a declaration in the middle of shooting an important motion picture. She called her mother in New York to confide their change in marital status before she read it in the newspapers or heard gossip. "I think this is something that's between Elliott and me, not the curious. We have to find out how things are between us and the less outside influence, the better," she answered columnist Dorothy Manners. [3-5-69 *L.A. Herald Examiner*] The writer later noted, "There's one thing I'll make book on: Barbra Streisand would never had left Elliott Gould if he had been down on his luck." Recognizing his impending potential, Streisand frankly raved about the man's looks in the coming months, "He is so handsome-- has such wonderful hair and that beautiful cleft in his chin. Jason has it, too, and I'm so happy about that." [Quoted 7-70 *British Photoplay*]

Although the Goulds were separated, they still lived together when he made *Bob & Carol & Ted & Alice* with Natalie Wood, Robert Culp and Dyan Cannon. The Goulds' amiable "trial separation" included her husband's continued representation of her business activities, and the actress hoped to star in a film possibly produced by Gould in his new Universal production deal. Reporters suggested that Streisand clung to her husband, reluctant to part from her psychological buffer, business partner, loyal friend, devoted lover and father of their son.

It was awkward to encounter each other at public functions, where all eyes followed their reunions. The actor had been uncomfortable with the pompous formality of the 1969 Academy Awards and very self-conscious escorting the woman from whom he had already separated. He knew many people would gossip and speculate because of their appearance together, a most traumatic evening for him. "I went to give support to Barbra, which made me ambivalent about what I was trying to prove and to whom." [11-70 *Playboy*] The husband admitted he never would have attended except that she had asked him to escort her, despite their recent estrangement. After the excruciating ceremony he vowed never again to escort her publicly, the couple learning to choose obscure locations for their get-togethers, preferring their son's company with them to defuse any awkwardness.

Two weeks after beginning her final Vegas engagement at the Hilton International in the 1971-1972 holiday season, Streisand's son's half-sister Molly was born to the new Mrs. Elliott Gould. Streisand was pleased that her ex-husband had found a woman so compatible and well-suited, a domestic type who sought only to provide a home to her man, which the first wife recognized as necessary for her former spouse. "Elliott and I were too competitive to have a long lasting happy marriage. There were too many influences outside. I was pushing, he was pushing. Our marriage wasn't an end in itself.

But I don't like talking about our marriage. I think the world is probably tired of hearing about it." She loathed her personal problems being so thoroughly analyzed, and traces her media shyness to that daily dissection of her marriage. [4-72 *Photoplay*]

The husband confessed, "It doesn't annoy me when I'm asked about her. I understand that it makes good reading. I'm interested in the social significance of it, y'know, but I'm not defensive about it." When asked about stress, he wittily gave the matter a new perspective, joking with the interviewer, "Well, when I relax, I get into my wife's clothing." [Quoted 5-69 *Coronet*] To him their relationship had been a match with two people sensitively tuned to the other's moods. Their separation was an undramatic gradual split, a tentative farewell.

Their first love had been based on deep, mutual trust, Streisand revealing her vulnerability to the man she loved-- but being so unhappy with herself, it was nearly impossible to develop true understanding of her husband's woes. He felt that she was suspicious of his need for her sympathy and under-standing, but friends would later explain that it would have required incredible sensitivity for a wife to cope with her hus-band's unique problems. "Even when people would call me Mr. Streisand I knew they were making a natural mistake. The whole situation was like the plot of an old B-movie, but I've never allowed myself to take it very seriously." [Quoted 10-70 *Pageant*]

Gould has also been quoted elsewhere, "What I gave her was more strength than was healthy for me. I taught her how to survive before I knew how to live." He insisted, "You can be brilliant and still understand nothing, I tell Barbra. It is like having ten million dollars but not a cent for a cup of coffee. In theory she has all the power in the world. In fact she is being used as much as anybody but she doesn't understand that."

Elliott Gould agreed to what would become an infamous interview for the August 1969 *Ladies' Home Jounal*, which the editors published as a "Funny Girl and Me" monologue. Gossip columnists and movie magazines widely reprinted the remarkable revelations about the marriage, his candor reverberating throughout Hollywood. The actor observed that like many unhappy marrieds, their relationship could have been prolonged another two decades without ever resolving their differences. They had speculated about parting for years, one such experiment failing because of their very real inhibitions and lack of confidence. "I don't think Barbra can help me. Barbra is really 14 years old. Her problem is not only that she has been swept off her feet by phenomenal success. It is more than that. It is what she thinks about herself." The star's husband felt that she would never be self-assured about her appearance and abilities no matter how many people rhapsodized about her.

He admitted how tiresome it was to have a wife so desperately discontented and therefore so thoroughly preoccupied with herself, always griping. "Barbra's favorite subject is Barbra," he complained. "It bugs me a lot, and I get bored by it sometimes." Gould felt that she did not know why she was unhappy, which caused her even more problems. He had lost patience with an important, beloved star who was so miserable in her personal life, who wore on his nerves with her endless fretting. His advice had been for her to undergo concentrated psychotherapy (as he had benefitted from daily analysis)-- or that on her own she should determine what was causing her despair and then hope to reconcile the discontent.

He half-jokingly suggested she could always accept her unhappiness in stoic quietness "...and be happily miserable." Without knowing the source of one's troubles, the result was "compulsively" keeping busy just to avoid oneself. "I would never envy Barbra her success. Her outer achievements allow her to avoid her inner problems, and this makes life bitter for her." Knowing what a fundamentally good person his wife is, he deeply regretted her frustrating dissatisfaction.

He was glad that he had kept a sense of humor about the label "Mr. Streisand," although he did resent the myriad falsehoods, such as the insinuation that his wife had financed his Broadway musical *Drat! The Cat!* to buy him a show, because they had actually invested only $750 each. Being unprepared for her achievements and having to live day-to-day with such a major star had only made him submerge his own identity. "Maybe I am guilty of copping out when I say, `If I didn't attend to our marriage, there would be no marriage.'" He even speculated that he took advantage of the personal situation to avoid the possible failure in not being able to find work; lacking the belief in himself that he could give his wife anything as an independent success, he devoted his time to her and her career. "I hated Barbra supporting me. It is essential for a man to support his woman."

Reading the husband's rambling conversations, it is obvious their relationship was doomed-- no man has the right to deny his wife her work to satisfy his fragile ego. He wanted to support her himself, and presumably the world would have sacrificed a Barbra Streisand, which seems to indicate not just a delicate but an insufferable ego. He could not and did not identify with her supreme ambition.

"Barbra and I had quite an unpleasant time the last several years-- with moments of loveliness." They believed that having a baby would stabilize their marriage, as they had been told, and their relationship was never better than when she was expecting their child. Finally able to relax, freed of her fears of getting fat, her femininity blossomed. They learned natural childbirth techniques, and he coached her daily in the breathing exercises, but unfortunately, a troubled breech birth meant that she was kept in the intensive-care unit for 24 hours. He reflected, "... Jason must not be the salvation of Barbra Streisand Gould. A baby should never be the salvation of a woman or a man." After the separation he worried about his son's being raised in a house of women, such live-in employees as the nanny, housekeeper and secretary. He feared that Jason was being prematurely taught manners and refinement, preferring for their son to be able to dirty the house, if he so desired, without being restrained or overly pampered.

Gould described his wife as ambivalent toward him, part of herself dependent upon her husband, the other half a scornful rival. "She has a problem that she can't reconcile-- that men are no good and can't be trusted. My adoration for her caused her to lose respect for me, to think less of me." Gould believed that his wife could not accept a man's affection when she did not like herself. "Barbra mistrusts anyone who needs anything from her." He hesitated to reveal to his wife what was troubling him lest she think him weak, although he overcame that inhibition after they were separated. He wished that more "respect and understanding" had benefitted their union, although he had not realized how unsympathetic he had been to the special problems of her being Barbra Streisand. "Barbra is an incredible animal-- she brings all of her personal pain and torture to her dressing room. Her work is the safest place for her."

Gould concluded, "Barbra and I might get together again... If we ever get back together, it has to be under enormously different terms... People who genuinely care about Barbra and me would like us to make it. But, honestly speaking, I doubt if we will." It is quite likely that speaking for this public forum was therapeutic for the alienated husband, able to express the feelings toward his wife which he was unable to do so directly. He seemed to accept that if she was public property, he could discuss her as such, but their relationship was damaged by the controversial feature.

Perhaps the bitter interviewee was stoned or drugged, but he later complained that he had been quoted out of context, his words distorted. He felt betrayed that a supposed friend had turned an article about acting into the seemingly anti-Streisand monologue. "...I worry about the press using me to get at Barbra. Especially using fallacious things. Like there was a piece in the *Ladies' Home Journal* quoting me as saying `Barbra is really only fourteen years old,' and things like that. That was a tasteless piece of rubbish. It upset Barbra. And the quote wasn't true." [Josh Greenfield interview] "The whole thing was the biggest put-on in life. The writer was my friend... she was supposed to be talking to me about my career. The story is totally unrealistic and misquoted. It made Barbra very upset. My friends have told me since that's one of the prices you have to pay in this business. I wouldn't have minded so much if it had been in a movie magazine. That's the kind of trash they print."

It was later in the first year of their separation, and Gould generously allowed:

I care deeply about her. We have a very deep personal relationship. We're no longer trying to save our marriage. What we've saved is our relationship. What we've gotten is a nice working relationship, which we didn't have before. My friends ask me if I think I'm a better actor now that we've separated. I think I'd be a jerk to say yes. I made `Bob and Carol' while I was still living with Barbra. That was the direct breakthrough or the emancipation of my success. [10-5-69 *N.Y. Times*]

The couple were still technically married when *Time* magazine featured the actor on the cover in September 1970, the wife remarking: "He did help me a lot when we were married, but mostly he kept my feet on the ground. At the same time, I wasn't considerate enough of his problems." Although Gould stressed the good as well as the bad in their marriage, Streisand observed, "It must have been very difficult for him. Marriages between people who are self-involved is hard. It's safer for actors not to be married to one another." This advice she has followed, until today a single woman, most of whose romances have been with non-actors and younger men. Gould is a couple of years older, while both Jon Peters and Richard Baskin are a couple of years younger.

After *Bob & Carol & Ted & Alice* made Gould a movie star, it must have a particular, proven pleasure for Streisand to attend the *M\*A\*S\*H* premiere with him, even though they had been separated for months. She must have been doubly impressed that her husband was validating the dramatic non-musical productions which she coveted, but exhausting himself with back-to-back films, the appearance was that of a man striving to match his wife's success with an excessive output of work. Although he continued to be a major American actor, this initial rash of success was to be his peak.

In 1970, with both parents living on the east coast, the Goulds aimed for one day a week spent with their son, often taking picnics to Central Park, such as during the New York filming of the actor's movie *Move*. When the woman was a frequent visitor in the early spring 1970 to her estranged husband's set, rumors of a marital reconciliation swept the gossip pages. In a mood of self-pity the actor told columnist Earl Wilson, "I am Barbra's friend, but she can't be my friend. She doesn't understand me. I have been her friend even before I saw her." A few months later he affirmed, "We're friends. She admits she doesn't understand me very good. And that's very possible!"

Gould began living out of wedlock with the beautiful daughter of film director Paul Bogart. The nineteen-year-old Jennifer was four months' pregnant with the first of their two children, Jason's half-sister and half-brother, when the Goulds received the quicky divorce in the Dominican Republic after 2½ years of separation.

While still months before he divorced Barbra Streisand, *Playboy* conducted an in-depth interview with Elliott Gould many years before the woman's own such dialogue. Gould was 32 in November 1970, and today he is approaching fifty. He confessed that he and his alienated wife did not agree on much but that they did respect and care for each other. He considered his spouse very special to him, but they both recognized the difficulties of wedlock. "Getting married imposes something technical on on otherwise viable relationship, and this often changes things drastically." They did not understand marriage and because they were so dependent upon each other, he believes they were both very brave to part.

They were still avoiding the pain of the final break, worse than "...the shame and embarrassment of saying, `Well, let's not live together anymore.' It's admitting failure. I wish people weren't so interested in this subject; their interest only helps add to my self-consciousness about it." Anticipating divorce as their only resolution, he was unhappy because of his still-high esteem for their relationship. "We communicate. But it's hard, man. It's really hard. I've changed a lot, you know, and so has my life." He was delighted to have found a woman completely unambitious and non-materialistic who was compatible with his simple lifestyle and pastoral ideology, and he was much happier and far less anxious than before. The man easily adapted to living with an unwedded mate, knowing the best times with his ex-wife had been before they were married, living together not because they were bound to each other but because they chose to do so.

Discussing his *Getting Straight* role, Gould said the director Dick Rush motivated and encouraged him to try something new. "Like the transition in the master's oral examination, where Bailey [his character] turns on the professors examining him. That was so wild-- a man getting it rammed up his behind, struggling with himself to fight back and finally winning... [Barbra] thought I was terrific. I know the film upset her, but she was moved by it. She's very critical and bright, and when it comes to acting, she's got a great eye.

So I was very pleased by her reaction. But it must be somewhat shocking to her to see me do things on the screen that she perhaps didn't know existed."

The Goulds' legal separation agreement in early 1971 granted each spouse the right to file for divorce after two years, but a few months later Streisand was dating Ryan O'Neal-- their comedy project already announced-- and Gould was living with the youthful Jennifer Bogart who became pregnant, which necessitated a speedy Dominican Republic divorce of the Goulds. Their separation announcement had been international news, much more so than when they quietly divorced 2½ years later. They were the first celebrities to become temporary seven-day citizens as a formality for an easy overnight divorce under the Caribbean island's month-old laws, on the grounds of "mutual consent." A local attorney represented the wife, with the husband present and accompanied by the nineteen-year-old Jennifer Bogart, who was five months pregnant with their child.

The quickie 24-hour divorce decree was granted on July 9, 1971 in the Santo Domingo civil court, the actor telling reporters, "If I see Barbra, I'd give her a kiss." Gould subsequently married his second helpmate soon after. The newly-unencumbered Streisand began freely dating Ryan O'Neal, but having endured many months of agonized indecisiveness about a divorce, fearful of the effect on their son, she sought increased refuge in psychoanalysis. Ironically, Gould blamed psychiatrists for the destruction of their marriage: "Analysts imposed themselves into the relationship before we even knew what we were doing." [6-29-80 *Washington Star*]

Optimistically hoping for a reconciliation when they had first legally separated, the Goulds did save their relationship but forfeited the marriage. Gould felt that although their love was undeniable, he and she lacked the proper ingredients of a successful marriage. When people wondered if the still-close friendship between Elliott Gould and Barbra Streisand could be resurrected again in marriage, the actress retorted in 1973, "I think once a relationship is dead, that's it, you can't revive it again." [8-73 Mary Kaye interview] Even without their son in common, they would likely have remained close, Streisand said. As she realized, "...how many people does one love in a lifetime?" Gould's update, six years later: "Sure, I still love her and we'll always be friends. You never really stop loving your first love, do you?" [6-79 *Films Illustrated*]

In 1973 the former husband had declared: "I recently read something Barbra said that pleased me very much. She said we would always be part of each other. She really is a remarkable person. You know something? She don't even listen to the radio! She don't know what's going on in the world-- she don't know who Al Green is, and she's never heard the Temptations sing, and I just know she's going to love my saying that about her. But the truth is she's come a long way." [3-4-73 *N.Y. Times*]

"Barbra and I will always be drawn together because of our mutual love for our son Jason... We know each other well and we have mutual respect. I can't imagine my life without Barbra as an essential part of it." [11-11-73 *L.A. Herald Examiner*]

The Goulds' offspring has not suffered from a bitterly broken home, having a very attentive father as well as a supportive "stepfather" of sorts in Jon Peters. At busy times during the mid-70's, the youngster stayed with his father through the week and with Streisand and Peters on the weekends. Asked if this situation pleased all the parties, Gould called the essential element understanding, accepting the separations stoically as he knew Jason was loved and protected with his mother. As for the substitute parent: "I have no reservations about Jon Peters. But I have no reservations for Jon Peters, either, which you can read any way you please." He did say that so long as his ex-wife is happy, Jason would benefit. [6-76 Guy Flatley interview/Quoted *Viva*]

The humiliating, ego-destroying identity crisis as "Mr. Streisand" seems to have endured as a painful part of the Gould character, and half-a-decade later his sensitivity to the issue of being the superstar's former husband was still apparent. At a large Hollywood party of country musician Kinky Friedman, the host and two rowdy guests-- Bob Dylan and Art Garfunkel-- followed Gould around warbling the lyrics to "People," which so incensed the actor that he pronounced Dylan a "four-foot, two-inch Jewish Prince" and was finally escorted out the door. [4-22-76 *Rolling Stone*]

After divorcing for the second time, the actor wondered, "Why can't I have a lasting relationship with a woman? It stems from my upbringing, I'm sure. My parents stayed together when they shouldn't have, when it was dishonest to do so, and that affected me greatly." [5-24-79 *L.A. Times*] He has said that one of his personal problems was in not being able to be friends with a female.

Elliott Gould worked on his autobiography for several years, and in spring of 1981 he announced that he was refusing all publishing offers, intending the memoirs to be a personal heritage for his three children. "If it is ever to be published, it will be a family decision. If they don't like what I've written, I'll just put it away and forget about it." [4-28-81 *L.A. Times*] He compared the style of his tale to that of the novel *Ragtime*-- in which his life would be set against a background of historical events-- but the memoirs would focus very little upon his first marriage. "You know what Barbra would say to me? `I'll trust you that it will be the truth. You be the judge but if you have any doubt, I'm never going to let you do it, no matter what.'"

Streisand recalled on the 1983 *20/20* documentary, "[Elliott] was very bright, very sweet, kind. I'm glad he's Jason's father 'cause Jason has a lot of his good qualities." The day following the telecast of her kind words, Gould told a reporter that she is "much more than an ex-wife to me." The actor's up-and-down, up-and-down, up-and-down career is now focused upon stage performing as well as television, with an occasional film role. One truth is certain: since Elliott Gould a second "Mr. Barbra Streisand" has never existed.

# Chapter 5

"The Favorite Role of Being
a Young Mother with a Young Son"

As a new mother, Barbra Streisand thoroughly objected to journalists' "putting a price tag on the rarest work of art, like a miracle" after her pregnancy had caused her to cancel a million dollars' worth of concert bookings in 1966 and the press had inevitably labeled her child "the million dollar baby." So that the public and the press would not gape at her infant's bassinet, she had listed him as the son of Angelina Scarangella, her onetime alias. She worried about the pressure on Jason Emanuel Gould of being the son of not one but two famous parents.

Knowing she would have to let an adult son go, she intended to enjoy Jason as much as possible when he was young, but the mother felt that she had no right to expect her son to heed her expectations: "They didn't ask to be born, and they don't owe you anything unless they want to." She had anticipated the birth of a daughter but instantly fell in love with her son and hoped to have more children sometime in the future. "I'd like a girl next, but I was very glad that I had a son first," she said when Jason was nearly four. She was grateful that he enjoyed his food because she did not force him to eat, unlike her own upbringing, when her mother had been so preoccupied with food. [4-69 *Good Housekeeping*]

Streisand was proud that her son conversed beyond mere baby talk. "He's so open, he knows so much, and he's uncorrupted by phony attitudes. I don't want to put my own crap in his head anymore than I can help, but I'm resigned to the fact that there's no way I can not screw him up." She recalled: "... we're on an elevator and I say `Why didn't you say hello to that man, didn't you see how unhappy you made him?' He said `I used it up, I already used up all my hello's today.' So I tried to explain that hello's and goodbye's are, well, unlimited. He said, `Mother, in my difference, I don't like to say hello's and goodbye's.' `In my difference'... a beautiful concept, don't you think? Such a sense of self, and childhood, and adultness, all at the same time." [6-24-71 *Rolling Stones*]

Elliott Gould: "Barbra is a Jewish mother who goes to pieces when Jason sniffles." The father kept their child during the month of August 1971 when Streisand was filming *What's Up, Doc?* in San Francisco, although she had isolated herself at home with him for a year-and-a-half before filming the comedy, keeping very busy with a domestic life she enjoyed. Rather than an overdoting, blind affection, the mother meant to have a meaningful relationship with her boy. When he was only five, she was pleased that he accompanied her on her travels, although she accepted that when he started school she would have to leave him at home--but not for long periods, she swore. She feared being overly protective and loving the boy too much, aware that she would then be baffled by any kind of misbehavior from her offspring. The mother also recognized that it was wrong to sacrifice everything for him. "Living for your children is deadly if that's all you're doing."

Although it appalled her to break the news about her separation from his father, she finally realized the truth would work the best. He accepted her assurances that his parents would be more content apart and that he could visit with his father as much as he wanted. She never meant for any of the men in her life to fill a father's role in her son's life; when she was heavily involved with Ryan O'Neal, she meant for him to be friends with her son, just as she said she was not a mother figure to his children. [4-72 *Photoplay*]

During *The Way We Were* filming, the actress arose at a painfully early hour to be able to return home in time to put her son to sleep, and when she was forced to stay at work, she accepted the traditional dictum that the quality of time compensated for the quantity of hours a parent spends with a child. When she kept her son awake later than his bedtime so that they would have more time together, the mother worried that that she was letting her work schedule interrupt his health and rest. They enjoyed each other's company at these times, but she still fretted as she justified her actions. "Honestly, though, my own childhood was pretty awful." [8-73/Mary Kaye interview]

Elliott Gould's son appeared as four separate juvenile cameos in his father's *Harry and Walter Go to New York*; his debut role had been at the age of five in another film failure, in his mother's *Up the Sandbox* merry-go-round ride.

That Barbra Streisand is quite an enthusiastic mother who delighted in her son's education and in their mutual camaraderie is obvious. She has bragged about his sense of humor. She described how Jon Peters spent time with the boy, a substitute or part-time father helping the boy overcome his childhood fears; Jason had the kind of teacher the actress regretted not having had as a child. Streisand had always felt that motherhood was for other people, somehow, that she was not meant to have a child, as though something were wrong with her. Then she marveled that a tangible person whom she conceived and to whom she gave birth who was now able to write music, and she contemplated using one of his songs in *A Star Is Born*. [11-76 *L.H. Journal*]

Streisand enjoys the unique perspective of the world her offspring has given her. Instead of feeling guilt for not being able to spend more time with her teenage son, she finally realized she is who she is and tried to make him realize how crucial her career is to her.

# Chapter 6

## "A Wistful Relationship
## with Burt Bacharach"

In retrospect it seems possible that the spark of genesis for the "Lost Inside of You" songwriting scene from *A Star Is Born* originated not only during the true-life incident with Leon Russell but half-a-decade prior during the March 1971 Burt Bacharach television special on which Barbra Streisand guested. The composer was young and handsome and the woman was single and eligible. Although Bacharach was married, the attraction between him and the superstar performer as they stared into each other's eyes is subtly erotic. Streisand looked marvelous and the man's wife was said to be seething.

When dueting together, the guest's reverential appreciation was quite evident, but Bacharach explained to reporters that it was the director's idea for her to hang over the piano, adding a special feeling to the program. Movie magazines avidly devoured the possibilities of a rift in the musician's marriage, purporting that actress Angie Dickinson was jealous of Barbra Streisand, the wife questioning the inordinate amount of time spent with the special guest.

With a split-screen camera and overdubbing trickery, Streisand was able to duet with herself as she sang the composer's "A House is Not a Home" in a first-time medley with his "One Less Bell to Answer" (lyrics to both by Hal David). When Bacharach joined her at the piano, the pair sang the familiar hit song "Close to You" as it has never been sung before, then Streisand sang an original composition written expressly for her, "Be Aware," in which a sensitive artist expressed concern for a world lulled by luxury while the other half languish in suffering and deprivation, an ultimate message song for the singing actress. She told the composer how especially nervous she was "singing the song before the man who wrote it," but her performances were particularly well received.

# Chapter 7

## "BJS"

Critics as well as fans were mystified by the separate spellings of *Barbara Joan Streisand* and *Barbra Joan Streisand* on the front and back covers of her self-titled August 1971 album. The singer furthered the confusion by smiling on thephoto which depicted the original version of her name, which perhaps explains the motive: a kooky Barbara, a serene and somber Barbra... A good interview question would ask why the stark photography shows a pensive cover in sharp focus and titled *Barbra Joan Streisand*, alternated with the fuzzy back-cover photo of a smiling singer.

The original pressing of this album featured a large poster of the cover intended to decorate the walls of the singer's burgeoning fans. Having tried in vain with her *What About Today?* album to tap the mushrooming youth market and then succeeding with a vengeance on the subsequent *Stoney End* single and album, the singer returned to the producer, Richard Perry, who had helped her deliver a gold album featuring the works of Laura Nyro and other contemporary composers. A year after first inaugurating a new modern sound, she began recording a third album in early June 1971.

*Barbara Joan Streisand* debuted in the Top 40 and was the singer's eleventh $1,000,000 gold album seller by December of 1971. Released late that year and coinciding with her Las Vegas International holiday season engagement, the half soul/half pop album was a watershed recording in the career of the extraordinary songstress, masterfully blending the old Streisand with the new-- ballads and rock numbers seamlessly joined-- expanding the contemporary move she had already successfully mined. The singer was accompanied on some arrangements by organist Billy Preston; Clydie King and Vanetta Fields were background vocalists who would be featured as the Oreos in *A Star Is born*; Fanny, the all-female Warner Bros. rock group, also joined Streisand on certain cuts.

Streisand sang the Burt Bacharach-Hal David medley she had premiered on the composer's March 1971 television special, the self-duet "One Less Bell to Answer" with "A House is Not a Home" being one of the singer's shining moments on vinyl. The much-recorded Carole King standard "You've Got a Friend" became a Streisand song on her *Barbara Joan* LP, as well as "Where You Lead" with choral backup by the future Oreos. The songwriter's "Beautiful" made three *Tapestry* songs which Streisand covered--one-third of the famous album.

Only a scant few acts have reached the Top 40 with both a studio and a live version of a song, one of which is Streisand's "Where You Lead" from this album and the Grammy-nominated live medley of "Where You Lead" and "Sweet Inspiration" from the *Forum* concert album.

Despite the encouraging results of *Stoney End*, critics complained of the follow-up album that the highly-refined Streisand style overpowered the contemporary songs, but it seems a subjective matter. Although some reviewers were opposed to the eclectic mixture, an album should not have to be totally unified anyway, contrasted selections even more effective in reaching a broader audience. Most critics appreciated the evolving Barbra Streisand, and the album and single "Where You Lead" were both hits, although not as successful as *Stoney End* and its title song 45.

*BJS* benefitted from the lessons of a forerunner recording and presented the kind of material the singer could master.

The beautiful ballads were incomparable, the emotional feeling really noticeable as she lilted through "Since I Fell for You," a brilliant torch number similar to her early-career material. Her voice is spritely and spirited on "I Never Meant to Hurt You," genuinely hurt by the other's pain. Steely Dan's Donald Fagen and Walter Becker wrote "I Mean to Shine," an excellent example of Streisand as a contemporary pop artist. John Lennon's "Love" was a soft gentle version of the lullaby and "Mother" was given a gospel-like rendition of Lennon's song with an element of pain alleviating the harsh bitterness of the rejected child. When producer Perry had given the singer John Lennon's solo LP, he was startled that she chose the hard-edged realism of "Mother," being drawn to the pretty melody despite the grittier rock than her two predecessor albums.

Clydie King and Vanetta Fields sang backup on Mathew Moore's spacey song "Space Captain," a Joe Cocker tune about an astronaut, although reviewers resisted the powerful Streisand voice singing the lightweight lyrics. The album's modern sound was offset by the softer melodies, such as "The Summer Knows," the latter number considered totally Streisandesque, a pleasing blend of lush Legrand music and the singer's dramatic rendition. The wailed, bluesy torcher by Buddy Johnson, "Since I Fell for You," included the slightest mournful echoes of its original countryish sound.

*Barbara Joan Streisand* sold very well, peaking at #11 on the charts. "Where You Lead" backed with "Since I Fell for You" was the first single, released two months prior to the album and reaching #3 on the Easy Listening charts but just cracking the Top 40 lists at #40.

*High Fidelity* critic Morgan Ames revealed his own brand of insight that young music followers today have no feelings good or bad for Rodgers and Hart type of music, theatrical music merely not relative to their tastes. "To say that this is a `new Streisand' implies that she has shed an old self. Yes and no-- mostly no. What this album displays is an alive and growing Streisand. Because of that, she will appeal most to the young and to those with open and still-growing minds. Naturally that means you." [12-71 *High Fidelity*]

# Chapter 8

"Finally Moving into the
Pop/Rock Mainstream with *Stoney End*"

In 1969 CBS Records met with lukewarm success as it eased Barbra Streisand into the modern mainstream of pop and rock music with her *What About Today?* album. Produced by Wally Gold, this first contemporary effort was disappointing, only reaching #31 on the charts and never certified gold. No smash Streisand albums had been heard in several years, the performer concentrating on her film career while the recording industry was undergoing such an upheaval.

The modern music movement demanded that the singer express herself in an instinctive, natural sense and with simple emotion, characteristics considered long obscured by Streisand's highly-polished and dramatic recordings. After a brief return to standards, releasing several singles which were only semi-successful, she was urged by her label to try another contemporary album after the misfired *What About Today?* The singer rebelled, reportedly interested in an LP of Bessie Smith songs, after having become exposed to the famed blues vocalist.

Then, early in the summer 1970, Streisand was to record another conventional album of serious music tentatively titled *The Singer*, with three songs from the Legrand-Bergman team. "Pieces of Dreams," the Oscar-nominated film song, as well as "Summer Me, Winter Me" and "What are You Doing the Rest of Your Life?" were recorded. She especially loved the latter ballad which she urged the Bergmans to convince director Richard Brooks she should record as the theme song to *The Happy Ending*, but he refused, insisting that it be an anonymous male voice. Released in April 1970, the "What are You Doing the Rest of Your Life?" single was only moderately successful, but Streisand persevered with *The Singer* album.

Hoping to persuade her to record more tunes of today, CBS mogul Clive Davis proposed specific material, seeking assistance from modern maestro Richard Perry, who suggested such songs as Harry Nilsson's "Maybe" and Randy Newman's "I'll Be Home." A meeting was arranged between the producer and performer at her Los Angeles home and she agreed to record the songs, being promised that if she were uncomfortable with the results, the tapes would be erased. The singer trusted, instinctively or methodically, the accomplished contemporary producer for this second attempt-- and successful transformation-- to master the modern sound.

Richard Perry's difficult challenge was to overcome the singer's inhibitions about the musical transition, especially after she had already tried and failed. The onetime Warner Brothers music producer felt that *What About Today?* was indeed current but too alike the traditional Streisand treatment, and he persuaded the uncertain singer about the merits of a genuinely contemporary recording. She was intimidated by the threat to her identity, and Perry realized that the singer had to create her own style of pop music without trying to imitate those other successful pop queens. He made her feel more natural, relaxing her discomfort, later disclosing to music biographer Shaun Considine that he introduced her to the pleasures of marijuana to loosen her inhibitions.

Although Streisand agreed to record an entire album, the jittery performer balked the night before the first recording session, protesting that she just did not identify with the material. He adamantly pleaded with her to trust him, and the next day, late in July 1970, she recorded her first genuine rock songs, "Maybe" and "I'll Be Home," followed by the album's eventual Laura Nyro title number, "Stoney End," an uptempo but medium-paced rock song featuring poignant lyrics the performer could dramatically enact, singing in an upbeat style about downbeat thoughts.  When they heard the three songs, she was pleased to have been wrong about rock-and-roll.

It is known that they continued to record for a record number of hours, from 7:00 p.m. to 5:30 a.m.  Five songs-- half an album-- were completed in the one session, including Joni Mitchell's "I Don't Know Where I Stand," which the Bergmans had proposed, as well as "Just a Little Lovin'" by Barry Mann and Cynthia Weill.  Perry later sent the singer a finished version of the disc, but she was baffled why the background vocals were nonexistent, until he visited her home in New York City and explained that she had a defective speaker in her stereo.

"Stoney End" was chosen as the first single, but as could be expected, the Streisand song was snubbed by rock stations until after several weeks of proliferating sales ensured acceptance by programming directors, the smash 45 becoming the first Top Ten song for Streisand since "People" seven years before.  Backed by Randy Newman's "I'll Be Home," the late September 1970 single was a hit by the end of the next month, reaching #6 on *Billboard* and ensuring the pop artist legions of new young fans.  The single debuted at #73 on the Hot 100 chart but then dropped 20 places the next week, eventually jumping to the top with a special Streisand thrust.  It was the singer's opening in Las Vegas which was considered responsible for the reverse direction of the single's *Billboard* fate, program directors having been invited to see the singer's cabaret show-- and she also promoted the song with phone calls and letters to prominent disc jockeys.

Not until the song hit was an album actually finalized, Columbia shelving the album of traditional songs which she had recorded-- ironically later repackaged as the smash solo *The*

*Way We Were* album-- and then Streisand and Richard Perry recorded the remaining modern tunes, such as "Time and Love" and "No Easy Way Down," more material from Laura Nyro and Randy Newman, respectively.

The collaborators disregarded the kinds of elements which had created *What About Today?*, recording only the best songs of the current young contemporary composers and eliminating the somber messages and any campy parodies. With not only the Top Ten single but the singer's having tested the new material on her Vegas audience late in 1970, CBS Records then released various contemporary melodies for a *Stoney End* album.

For the record cover Perry brought two photographers to the desert near Las Vegas where the singer was appearing that holiday season. "Camouflage Productions" was the apt name of the designers and photographers of the album's quaint cover, deliberately different from the old-fashioned sophistication of her *What About Today?* fashion sitting. The elegant star was featured in a down-to-earth pose, dressed in black with a grim expression on her face and perched on an antique loveseat in the back of a dilapidated pickup with New York's familiar license plates, enroute to a desolate and rocky stoney end.

The folk-based rock album *Stoney End* was released in February 1971 and sold fast and well, peaking at #10 soon after release, gold in just over two months. "Time and Love" was a follow-up single faring less well than the first, the second Laura Nyro song stalling at #51. Clive Davis successfully promoted the album with an enormous $100,000 expenditure, emphasizing the singer's youth in rock publications and FM radio stations advertising, interpreting her apparent older status as coming from a veteran career packed with achievement. "And while other performers her age sing the songs of young composers to people even younger, Barbra sings them for everyone." The ads artfully proclaimed:

"A new album by a young singer. She was the kid with the boom voice and wild gestures. The kook who wore thrift shop clothes when they weren't in vogue, and smothered her steaks in sugar for everyone to see if stars ate like real people."

Publicist Lee Solters sought a *Rolling Stone* interview to promote the album further, the singer reaching a wider and younger audience than ever before. He used a connection with the rock bible's editorial offices, and Grover Lewis was dispatched to cover the new Barbra Streisand. The journalist later told Shaun Considine he felt that he was obviously being used to promote the singer's LP (as if that were at all unusual). He genuinely believed she was acting, her behavior all an artifice. It is a shame that the writer so misunderstood the artist whom he perceived as phony. Barbra Streisand and Grover Lewis were clearly incompatible personalities, and the latter admitted the fallout from the controversial article blacklisted him for months. The man was obviously anti-Jewish and out to deliver a defeat of one kind or another to superstar Streisand.

*Stoney End* opened the decade for the singer with a newly-developed modern following, the difference in her appeal being that she muted the famous Streisand dramatics. Critic Stephen Holden noted much later, "Most of its songs came out of the hip Brill Building school of pop-rock which Miss Streisand had until then completely ignored. The three Laura Nyro songs at the album's center combined primitive and urbane ingredients that accommodated Miss Streisand's emotionality, while they encouraged her to relax her phrasing more than she had ever done." [11-6-77 *N.Y. Times*]

Although the singer recorded two Randy Newman songs, another pre-judgment of the public taste, and Richard Perry had asked the songwriter to play keyboards on his own songs, the musician complained years later after having become well-known with his "Short People" success: "Her voice is amazing, a freak, very accurate. But she isn't comfortable singing with a backbeat, which you need with my songs." Streisand herself has admitted of the backbeat that it denies her the opportunity to indulge her instincts, forced to record identical takes with the heavy rhythm overly guiding her interpretation.

Reviewers qualified their praise for the album for its too-faithful versions of the original material, although others applauded the singer for vocally refining the songs more than the singer-songwriters had. The emotional glow we hear in Joni Mitchell's "I Don't Know Where I Stand" was appraised as exceeding the composer's own version. Streisand's longtime accompanist Peter Matz candidly complained himself that the material, although not uneven as *What About Today?*, was too similar to the inspiration. Matz has theorized that the singer deliberately duplicated the songwriters' original versions, afraid of being non-commercial otherwise.

# Chapter 9

"Streisand Speaks Easily in Las Vegas"

After her newsworthy July 1969 debut at Las Vegas' Hilton International engagement, Barbra Streisand returned in late November 1970 to the Riviera Hotel where she had been booked in the early years of her career. The Riviera reprise was the conclusion to her original 1963 contract when the opening act for Liberace was paid only $7,500 a week in contrast to her later café dates paying ten times as much. The late Joe Glaser, president of Associated Booking Corp., represented Streisand professionally and negotiated the return.

In 1963 a Glaser staffer had discovered the hot new singer in a Greenwich Village club and then Glaser convinced Harvey Silbert, the Riviera Hotel owner, to fly to New York to catch the act, and she was signed that evening for the booking. Having become a powerful performer in the ensuing years, Streisand's contract was typically re-negotiated, paying an extensively higher salary than she was to have received, the new figure kept secret but estimated at $75,000 a week for two weeks. She only fulfilled one of her two return commitments, the hotel probably settling for one superstar series as acceptable. The Vegas stand was postponed several times, her representatives pleading that from filming she was "exhausted and unable to fill the grueling engagement."

She was also obligated to appear again at the Hilton International, the luxury hotel she had opened eighteen months prior, both establishments paying upwards of half a million for a five-week combined booking. A nagging problem had originally developed when the Riviera resisted the rival International Hotel's signing their star, insisting that they owned her contract precluding any other café appearances. The Riviera threatened to file an injunction or to seek interference with the American Guild of Variety Artists, but the impasse finally just dissipated.

The International must have chafed eighteen months later when Streisand's triumphant mastery of the Las Vegas speakeasy circuit occurred not at the new hotel but at the Riviera, the singer finishing the long-overdue contract, then immediately moving to the International with an act so identical that many critics declined to re-review the show. Renting a home during the engagement, Streisand performed at the Riviera from November 27 to December 10, then continued at the International from December 13 to January 2, 1971.

Numerous celebrities were in attendance for the Riviera opening. Franco Zeffirelli flew to Vegas, pitching *As You Like It* as a prospective film project. The Italian director had flown from Rome, and to make the singer's opening, chartered a flight from New York City when the airline was delayed.

Pearl Bailey announced during her visit backstage, "I'm proud to call her my sister."

For the first two-week run the singer again insisted she present a simple but sensuous program, but no longer coolly aloof or self-consciously pretentious, the mellow approach succeeded in the considerably smaller and more intimate Versailles Showroom. It was noted that not only the audience but the singer herself appreciated the mutual warmth. She added an opening act to help break the ice, comedian Pat Henry. This Streisand booking was spared all the hype and rites of the earlier history-making appearance, and critics commended the simplicity and lack of gimmicks in her act. Entertaining audiences not only with superb singing but with her own brand of unusual humor, she varied the monologues and song leads, sometimes humorously, experimenting with her New York and kook image accents.

The first night at the Riviera she walked onstage timidly, but at the end, the audiences honored her with a standing ovation. The singer considered this opening show one of the best of her career, and critics agreed. She related a bit of Las Vegas history and her passion for antiques, her down-to-earth rapping between songs including some scripted patter. The performer seemed to utilize the strain of her stage fright for energy, but despite her disclaimer of nervousness in the tea-drinking scenario, her presentation was quite polished and confident. As the playdates toiled, she was no doubt more secure as a trendy performer due to having a hit single, "Stoney End," and she added other rock-and-roll and rhythm-and-blues material from her contemporary recording sessions to the standards repertoire.

Of fifteen songs total, Streisand was accompanied by the Eddie Kendricks Singers (three black women and Kendricks) on selected numbers. Her material was rugged and challenging and flawlessly delivered, the performance widely acclaimed for succeeding with difficult songs. Glowing reviews would welcome the special cabaret artist.

Opening on Thanksgiving Day, the singer made a timid entrance to a thunderous welcome, but despite her hesitation she found herself with less performance anxiety than before. She had not worked in fourteen months, and the visibly uptight woman relaxed when discussing her fears after her fourth song. "The last time I was here in Las Vegas I was kinda nervous. It wasn't stage fright exactly. It was a thing called... *Death*! I would stand in the wings, and my whole life would pass right before my eyes, but I want to tell you I've overcome this problem-- now I feel absolutely great. I'm not nervous at all now. I can't breathe-- but I'm not nervous." Professing to be totally calm, she shook as she poured tea.

During her discourse, she pulled a cigarette case from her clothes, lighting a fake yellow joint and passing it around to the audience, giving what would become a standard spiel about not indulging in booze or drugs so that she had to find other ways of relaxing. "No, I'm not nervous at all, but I'll tell you who's nervous." She glanced backstage. "The owner of this hotel is getting awfully nervous!" She would later just scoff at the establishment's shock over her behavior.

The marijuana joint she pretended to puff at the 1972 concert for McGovern had originated in this Vegas act, she later recollected:

> Anyway, since I get nervous in places like Vegas, it occurred to me to do this funny little routine-- actually telling the audience about my hangup. The point was, you shouldn't rely on emotional crutches. It was almost a sermon-- no crutches, people, crutches are a no-no. Then at the end, I'd take out a joint and light it. First, just faking it. Then I started lighting live joints, passing them around to the band-- you know. It was great-- it relieved all my tensions. And I ended up with the greatest supply of grass ever.
>
> Other acts up and down the Strip heard about what I was doing-- Little Anthony and the Imperials, people like that-- and started sending me the best dope in the world. I never ran out. Hmn... I wonder if I should tell that story. [6-24-71 *Rolling Stone*]

The singer changed the pace for her audiences by relating her version of Vegas history.

> I have found you can find great old relics in Las Vegas. I go out in the desert all the time looking for antiques. This place used to be a hotbed of history. The Mormons came in about 1837-- it's a fantastic place. Let me show

you what I found this morning. I take out this horse every morning after *Sesame Street*-- the hotel gives me this horse-- it's an old horse-- sway-back so I can recline, ya know? Watch out-- my skate key, don't let it fall out. I found this in the desert this morning. Probably it was dropped from an old covered wagon--ya know, a wheel hit a rock. It's an old button, and on it is painted the face of a lady, a portrait, painted on this button, see? Get out your specs-- squint-- and in those days they must have had people like button painters-- can you imagine-- that would have been a fast fifty dollars on *What's My Line?*--anyway, can you imagine this guy calling up a model agency-- `Hello, could you send me someone with a small face?'

"I found something else, too. It looks like an arrow-head, but it's not really. It's an Indian roach holder. It must have belonged to the Shoshone Indians who came her in 1835 for a pow-wow. Even then it was a big convention town. The Paiutes didn't get here until October of the next year. They were all sitting around the lobby of Caesar's Palace-- ya know-- getting high on peyote-- celebrating the second day of Succoth. This place, Las Vegas, was centered around a fresh water spring. All the people-- Kit Carson, General Fremont-- would come to drink. That spring is now under the Tropicana swimming pool. This place that we're in right now, holding this gathering, was once a sunken creek. It was the creek General Fremont made his famous retreat into in 1844. But, before it was a creek it was a river-- this whole area here was the river-area. [Laughter, applause] Ah, ah, that's why they must have named this hotel the Riviera. Ummm, they put two and two together, and you get five. That's what I heard anyway."

The orchestra began playing again, and when she sang the "Second Hand Rose" lyric "Even things I'm wearing, someone wore before!", Streisand noted wryly over her shoulder, "like hell!" She then sang a medley of Sophie Tucker songs, "A Good Man is Hard to Find" and "Some of These Days." She proclaimed, "Ya know, girls, when you play the game of love, you put your heart on the spin of the dice. And though the dealer may turn up the jack of spades, ummmm, let the chips fall where they may, girls, you paid the price. Yes, girls, what a woman's got to keep in mind, even though she may be the queen of hearts-- he may discard her. And though the next good man is mighty hard to find, a good woman is even harder." She returned to the stool and pleaded, "Won't someone please tell me the time? Have you noticed there are no clocks here? I go up to my room and the television set is broken, and the Bible only has five commandments."

She sang the plaintive "Happy Days Are Here Again," but for a three-way medley added a few lyrics from Judy Garland's "Get Happy," then seguing into the jubilant rock-edged gospel melody "O Happy Day!" as a finale. With the soulful Kendricks Singers as accompaniment, the effect was splendid on this happy conclusion, first bluesy and doubtful then traditional uptempo.

The sixty-minute concert at 8:00 p.m. was repeated each night at midnight. When a fan asked for "The Best Things You Ever Did," Streisand seemed baffled and told him, "You said that wrong, but at this hour I'll forgive you. You mean `The Best Thing I've Ever Done,'" when she actually meant "The Best Thing You've Ever Done." When a young fan screamed, "I LOVE YOU!", she thanked him but ignored the compliment when he said it again. After the third attention-getting shout, she paused and looked at him, "You said that already," and the youth was silent thereafter.

In an interview she analyzed her current engagement: "Last year I tried to create theatrical image. Now I'm just singing. But I easily bore myself and I don't like singing the same songs. I can't stand singing `People' anymore-- How can I impart a feeling? I really have to work hard at that-- not looking bored." Unconcerned about possibly forgetting the lyrics, in which case she would simply begin again, she felt more comfortable singing new material. The singer often brought the words onstage with her to ease her anxiety, finally able to abandon the crutch by the end of the engagement.

She worried about people's preconceived notions and misconceptions but finally insisted, "There's no image to uphold. I'm fallible. I'm human. I was so frightened last year. All I kept thinking about was what am I supposed to be. The moment I stepped out on stage I was in shock. It was like `what am I doing here?'" With a certain satisfaction she realized how petrified an audience member would be if he or she were called onstage to perform. [12-20-70 *L.A. Herald Examiner*] She has further explained her dislike of live performing as the loss of motivation which had fueled her as a novice teen eight years earlier.

One Tuesday night the singer taped a segment which was telecast December 22nd on a special programming called *A World of Love*, Streisand singing "The Best Gift" about the birth of a child. Her café shows had been shortened that night, some songs and the monologues deleted in order to perform for the cameras. At the Riviera closing night, Nevada Governor Paul Laxalt, later the powerful Republican Senator, telephoned to express his pleasure and admiration of the singer who was unable to accept his dinner invitation because she was hosting the crew's Chinese cuisine party in her dressing room. Elliott Gould, heavily-bearded and then in his film preeminence, anonymously attended the closing and afterwards visited with his then-separated wife.

The star received AGVA's "Best Female Entertainer of the Year" honor in 1970, as well as the following year. When Ed Sullivan presented the "Georgie" Award on a highly-rated special filmed at the International Hotel, the winner Barbra

Streisand agreed to appear when she was told she could plug any charity of her choice, choosing the retarded children's cause she supported.

A *Hollywood Reporter* critic complimented the singer, "It's possible to get so spellbound watching and listening to Barbra Streisand that at the end of one of 15 songs, one almost forgets to applaud. Marvelously simple, uncluttered and unfettered by gimmicks, Miss Streisand is more than deserving of the adoration and ovations she received from the audience. She's a very hip performer and makes her material and bits charming and entertaining."

* * *

After the Riviera run, Streisand's second Hilton International commitment immediately followed, three days later, these extended engagements in December 1970 requiring an extreme case of discipline. This second cabaret appearance was also to record crowds. One night toward the end of her stint, she heard a buzzing sound from an amplifier and asked the orchestra, "Is there a new sound on stage tonight, or is it just me?" When she was told the reason, she exclaimed, "Thank goodness! I thought it might be the pot. I was afraid that somebody slipped me the real stuff!"

She joked at one point during the performance that it was a good time for the audience to sit back and meditate: "I bet I could just slip away, and no one would notice," but when she tried to do so, the spotlight followed her. She pretended to be angry with the lightman, yelling, "So you're the one with all the power, huh?" All the lights were doused, and she yelled, "Not THAT much power!!"

She eliminated all the "crap" of the star build-up in Vegas, experimenting every time she appeared in concert. No "fancy gowns, no intro, no overture." She really did not care for such practices, considering them actually fraudulent to the audience.

"On top of which, I don't like to perform.  That's true.  I don't even like to be watched." [6-24-71 *Rolling Stone*]

# Chapter 10

"A Shaky Transition to a Modern Sound"

After Barbra Streisand's starburst recording prosperity, her studio album sales dipped for a bit as she concentrated on her film acting, but *What About Today?* marked a recording resurgence, although the contemporary sound never quite blazed with any hit singles or in the critical esteem, the album peaking at #31 and never certified gold. *What About Today?* seems to have gotten lost in the musical and social clamor about Woodstock, but the album marked an adjustment in the Streisand music career, an attempt as the title states to touch the contemporary pulse of protest performance: the conversion to the contemporary sound merely survival.

Playing to the very establishment older crowd at Las Vegas, the mantle of the mature woman with the traditional, old-fashioned repertoire was hardening in an era emphasizing youth. Dean Martin, Sammy Davis, Jr., Frank Sinatra, Tony Bennett and company were the young singer's counterparts in the casino showrooms with their audience of elderly blue-haired ladies and grey-headed companions. The young singer was astonished to be asked to perform in charitable concerts with performers such as the late Jack Benny, but the woman's older image was challenged by the success of *Stoney End* and later overcome for good with *A Star Is Born*. CBS Records gambled that Barbra Streisand would outdistance her easy-listening origins and not vanish with the Eydie Gormé, Peggy

Lee, Perry Como singers forced into retirement by the rock music revolution.

Streisand had agreed to attempt the modern sound but only songs with meaningful lyrics. In late January 1968, she recorded three songs with Jack Gold, in New York: the promisingly-titled "Our Corner of the Night," the lovely ballad "He Could Show Me," and "Frank Mills" from *Hair*. For the latter, music publisher Nat Shapiro introduced her to the song from the Off-Broadway musical which would become a Broadway smash, but she reportedly hesitated to release her version when she learned of the unique nature of the avant-garde musical revue, the performers totally disrobing on a nightly basis. In March she recorded two more current songs, "What About Today?" and "The Morning After," the lyrics, as was the trend during the late sixties, protesting injustice but with an old-fashioned musical arrangement, especially on the latter song.

*What About Today?* was over a year in the making, although haphazardly. Streisand dabbled with the contemporary package over a long period of months, just when her recording career was being neglected in lieu of Hollywood. "Our Corner of the Night" backed with "He Could Show Me" was released as a single in early 1968, the 45 receiving little promotion and less airplay. A whole year before the *What About Today?* album was ready, another single failed in April 1968, "The Morning After" backed with "Where is the Wonder?", the latter number resurrected from *My Name Is Barbra*. Then in early February 1969 CBS unsuccessfully released "Frank Mills," which was, like "Our Corner of the Night" and "He Could Show Me," never included on any LP, although the flipside song "Punky's Dilemma" would become an album cut on her upcoming first contemporary album. The fourth, and uncharted, single was in June 1969, "Little Tin Soldier" and "Honey Pie."

To assemble a full-length package of these contemporary songs for a mid-year 1969 album, a new producer was finally chosen, Wally Gold (not to be confused with Jack Gold, who delivered the first three singles), and recording began in late May in New York. Streisand chose some popular songs to cover, "Alfie," which Burt Bacharach had sent her, and "Until It's Time for You to Go" from Buffy Sainte-Marie. As if disregarding the modern writers and arrangements, the vocal performance was Streisand's usual theatrical interpretation. The repertoire was expanded with songs ranging from "Little Tin Soldier," a somber anti-war message, and a contemporary pop offering from Harold Arlen-- "That's a Fine Kind of Freedom," which the veteran songwriter had donated to the civil rights movement-- to rock, probably frustrating the label-conscious press.

The singer also included two Beatles songs, the touching innocence of "Good Night" and a giggly "With a Little Help from My Friends." Ex-Beatle Ringo Starr: "She once did `With a Little Help from My Friends,' and I loved it. It was off the wall and funny but not juvenile or self-indulgent." [Quoted by George Hadley-Garcia/*Barbra Now & Then* #4]

Three arrangers conducted the album sessions, the singer's reliable Peter Matz as well as Don Costa and Michel Legrand; the latter musician's enduring memory is of the singer's seventeen takes of "With a Little Help from My Friends." Once when studying her performances, she stopped the tape recorder after thirty minutes and sighed, "I'll have to stop. I'll have no voice left," dismissing the inevitable comment that she was only listening and not singing: "Maybe not, but I've been listening so hard I feel like I've done a two-hour concert!"

Two elegant period pictures on the covers ironically contrasted with the modern, youthful vein of the material, Streisand impersonating two meaningful theatrical roles irrelevant to the musical message. The front photograph was inspired by a noted study of Colette, the French novelist, and for the alternate look on the reverse side the singer posed for Richard Avedon in what must be one of her thrift-shop finds, an antique feather boa, a look meant to resemble her favorite actress, Sarah Bernhardt. The singer wrote a chic message for the liner notes (and was paid a $50 fee). Scribbling her signature, she signed a dedication to the concerned youth of the day.

> "This album is dedicated to the young people who push against indifference, shout down mediocrity, demand a better future, and who write and sing the songs of today. With my deepest admiration, Barbra Streisand."

As she would explain joining forces with her own generation, the new woman was affiliating with grass-roots organizations devoted to charitable and political concerns.

The experimental recording failed to impress the critics, who condemned the traditional treatment of modern material. Protesters argued that the Beatles pieces and Paul Simon's "Honey Pie" were meant to be rougher rock than the overly dramatic, cutesy versions rendered by Streisand, although some reviewers interpreted the pop treatment as deliberately avoiding identification with the composers' original versions. "Honey Pie" was meant to be a parody of an earlier era's movie songs, but the campy song with its cartoon character's Betty Boop voice and the rollicking piano and laughing and giggling were considered an anachronistic early-century flapper arrangement on the contemporary album.

Singing the album's incendiary lyrics in her fancy theatrical tradition failed to be inspiring or convincing to many critics, who reiterated that such a dynamo required dynamic songs; Streisand too easily subdued weak and amateur music as the light pop sound was regarded, regardless of the fact that the heated material was composed by very angry young writers. The reviewers also condemned what they considered contrived emotion on the album.

Streisand had dismissed the kind of the current material with which she was ill at ease, finally choosing the miscellany package of odds and ends gathered under the title *What About Today?*, almost answering her own question about the rock revolution.  Although the singer was trapped by the moguls' pressure to record music commercially meant to pacify the youthful revolution's peculiar time and mood, it is regrettable that both kinds of music could not have been deemed appropriate.

An Evart Alimine humorously dismissed *What About Today?* in the long-deceased tabloid *National Tattler*: "What it can be labeled is `incompossible', which means the state of being unable to exist if something else exists-- like Streisand's singing and God's mercy to man."  A contest was announced with a prize of the once-played-only *What About Today?* album. [11-16-69]

# Chapter 11

## "A Non-Musical X-Rated Film Comedy"

Barbra Streisand's fourth film, *The Owl and the Pussycat*, was her first non-musical, an initially X-rated 1971 comedy in which the actress starred as a "non-promiscuous" hooker opposite George Segal as a pseudo-intellectual, would-be writer. Bill Manhoff's 1964 Broadway comedy played for 429 performances in New York at the same time Streisand appeared in the neighboring hit show *Funny Girl*, and in 1966 the actress saw the two-character farce for the first time in London.

Although Ray Stark had an option on four more Streisand pictures after *Funny Girl*, the actress' ironclad contracts were with two other studios, so her second Rastar film waited until this fourth offering, a breach-of-contract suit amicably resolved with the actress' agreement to undertake the comedy and to settle with the producer for a salary of $1 million plus 7% of the profits. During the filming, as always, Stark fought with an actress who obviously resisted the producer's old-time control over actors. Their ambivalent relationship has been likened to a tempestuous marriage, in which the affection is as real as the hostility. Streisand admitted the Rastar picture was "an obligation to fulfill," but she also relished the role.

Playing a brassy but gentle-hearted hooker is an example of Streisand's duality: from three G-rated musical extravaganzas to an X-rated adult comedy. In the late 1960's Hollywood was changing to reflect the new perceptions of the socially and sexually relevant young audiences, and the new permissiveness thrilled and challenged the actress who had felt stifled by the family fare of her establishment, last-of-the-old-fashioned mammoth musicals. Freed of a species threatened with extinction, now she would be as modern and natural as she chose.

Streisand finally checked the trend of a singing actress starring in high-fashion film fantasies meant for general audiences, the reversal in one's public following from an older establishment crowd to a flock of youthful fans being unprecedented for an entertainer. *The Owl and the Pussycat* was a gamble in the sense of a phenomenal singer-actress disdaining the traditional musical format by expanding her performing abilities, but Hollywood commentators considered her relinquishing the opulent and expensive genre as wise and logical in an era of failing studios.

The producer planned to alter the film role to make Doris a struggling folk singer; desperately unsure about the singing actress' non-musical debut, Ray Stark hoped that Barbra Streisand songs would at least play in the background of the soundtrack. Both Streisand and Stark would win, the performer proving her ability to succeed without song and the film maker's capitalizing on her non-singing debut for publicity, exploiting the transition from singing roles to dramatic.

The producer had finally yielded to his star's insistence that she not sing in the comedy, but she still sounded bitter a few years later. Telling Stark that she did not want to sing, that it would be her first time just to act, she had been frustrated by his press announcement that she would perform two numbers. "Naturally, when the showdown came, I said there was no way I would sing. You see what I mean? I was pushed around. Made to feel like I was a bad little girl or something. There was no reason for that." [late 1972 *Newsday*]

Streisand accepted the non-singing gambit as she had taken risks all her working life, although she was baffled that she had to fight for everything. "People said, `You've got to sing in

*Owl and the Pussycat,'* and I said `I'm not going to sing,' and they said you can't not sing. I said I'm not only going to not sing, I'm going to not sing in at least four pictures." [5-75 *McCall's*] She desired a non-singing role in a non-formula film as a chance for creative excitement, the star's emotions about her singing quite contradictory after her musical beginnings. No more pictures "with the background in focus," she retaliated. [1-70 *Newsweek*] *The Owl and the Pussycat* was purposefully low-keyed and low-budgeted, a more personal picture meant to be a departure from the superstar's debuting megamusical trilogy.

Especially inspired by Elizabeth Taylor's "uninhibited" portrayal in *Who's Afraid of Virginia Wolf?* for which she deliberately made herself unattractive, the young actress welcomed the change in the direction of her career. The initial trio of musicals had been "real movies" fulfilling her childhood vision of screen stardom-- for her next role she would be without the lustre of wigs, dyes, and period costumes, Streisand planning to portray her basic self, "the me that's natural and very today." She sought to merge with her own age group, having felt all along "older somehow," hoping not to be so concerned as before about her appearance and entertaining the idea of presenting herself from all sides in a comedy. "Maybe there are more bad angles to me than good. I just want to be human." She admitted that her opinions wavered constantly, and cinematographer Harry Stradling expressed doubts that she would ever actually desire to look bad.

"It's such a shlep doing those big musicals-- it takes a year, a whole lifetime away from you, rehearsing, prerecording, fittings, etc. Now I can make a little movie in ten weeks, no songs, like a normal person. I mean, you do a movie and you go home." Her lessened work schedule in a smaller picture allowed her for the first time to discover the physical nature of her body, a sedentary creature eagerly embracing such sports as tennis and swimming. [12-16-69 *Look*]

Originally a black actress named Diana Sands had por-trayed Doris on Broadway, with Alan Alda playing the white man, but it was thought that reality suffered without a reference to the racial situation. In a color reversal, Stark considered the great Sidney Poitier for the writer's role, the script revised to include her First Artists partner. Streisand explained, "It will give it some social significance. Make it a little more impor-tant." A theme of miscegenation in those turbulent times would have been a welcome innovation in the Streisand film canon, but unfortunately Columbia Pictures feared that an interracial casting would alienate audiences.

After struggling to be given the co-starring role, Streis-and's Carolwood Drive neighbor Burt Reynolds would later admit how thwarted he had been to be rejected in favor of George Segal. A match with the eventual superstar actor would have been an intriguing Streisand co-star, but he would have been too virile for the bookish role. Segal was perfectly cast, a plausible choice who worked well with Streisand. He has marveled at the superstar's goddess-like charisma which she summoned at will: "I'd see her sitting on the set hunched up like a little old lady, looking about as glamorous as a head cold. But the minute she stepped in front of the camera-- Pow! She was a mega-star. And boy you knew it!"

In this marvelous comedy Doris Waverly's seldom successful attempts at modeling and dancing turn into selling herself for money, an occasional lady-of-easy-virtue whose rapid love-hate rollercoaster ride with Felix Unger would be critically acclaimed. It was an opposites-attract story, the rational owlish snob clashing with the earthy, emotional, uneducated and pussycattish "entertainer."

In adapting the stageplay for the widescreen, *The Owl and the Pussycat* was opened out by the masterful Buck Henry, who easily constructed a tale for the two actors already committed to the project. Especially crafting the fast-paced urban dialogue for the unique Streisand speaking voice, one of the wiser decisions was changing the locale from San Francisco to New York, and he urged an honest portrayal of a hooker's life and language. The actress overcame her natural reluctance to speak so graphically as well as acting whorish when she too determined to be genuinely shocking.

Then publicizing a series of celebrity character-study monologues analyzing the question "Who am I?", *Life* magazine asked Streisand to byline an article. She requested that the screenwriter critique her laboriously-fashioned rough draft, and Henry may have advised her not to be so honest to the extent that she would be exposed to criticism. She of course has always maintained an abiding compulsion to tell the truth, and the quite candid published article was well received.

Behind the camera for the actress' first four films and personally chosen by Streisand, the aging cinematographer Harry Stradling, Sr. died during the *Owl* production, the veteran's work completed by Andrew Laszlo. Streisand also requested Herb Ross as her director, the gifted man who had choreographed her musical sequences in *Funny Girl*. Ross: "There was a peculiar intimacy in the film with so few of us involved and we had to break down our inhibitions to do it. We rehearsed for two weeks before shooting, and got so loose, it was silly... we lay in bed together on the set and just laughed." [11-30-70 *Women's Wear Daily*] Ross recognized how valuable it was to the insecure actress to play a woman so many men find attractive.

After the actress flew to New York City to rehearse, filming soon began in November and was expected to finish in January 1970. It was the first and only time that Streisand filmed entirely in New York, on location on the East Side and in Columbia soundstages. Little negative publicity emerged from the set which had been closed at the actress' discretion, but she was said to hide in her dressing room when she was actually reserving free time for her son and for herself. The actress spent her solitude studying her newest pursuit, Proust.

Another current pastime was painting; she preferred abstract art at the time and covered her intricate manicure with plastic gloves. The star was said to have resisted all advice about clipping her long elegant nails to portray a prostitute, finally relenting on her own.

Comfortable with her total performance, Streisand was at ease working on this comedy. Admittedly lazy, she enjoyed a novel trend from her former obsession with trivial details. She was unusually punctual for each day's shooting and prided herself on the esteem from Ross and Segal, which was a mutual feeling, an earnest affection apparent. Being in her home city, she was also comfortable with the crew's accent, a sound compatible with her Brooklyn voice. Herb Ross: "I can't tell you how marvelous she's been. It all comes out sounding like platitudes, but she's so generous-- willing to do it my way or George's way. She has a feeling not that everyone loves her but that she's one of us." With the comic role the director discovered Streisand's deep capacity as a performer. "She's really what acting is all about-- being. The more she tests her range the more expanded that range is going to be." [1-10-70 *Newsweek*]

Director Herb Ross would later remember that although Streisand showed not a shred of inhibition onscreen, she had been quite intimidated by the offbeat role. Fan magazines reported the unsubstantiated tale that the actress researched her characterization by dressing anonymously in scarf and hat and, accompanied by a studio official a few steps behind her, observing the hookers procuring customers on Times Square. The story is dubious if for no other reason than its being the standard preparation for this kind of role. Whether true or not, for years the New Yorker would have noticed the whores along the "red-light district" of Broadway.

Doris' hilarious shortie nightgown with gawdy pink applique hands sewn over the cups and a welcoming heart placed over the crotch of her panties was a unique costume, and outdoors the hooker wore an equally vivid mini-skirt, white go-go boots and a fake fur coat. The actress' mother was a surprise and surprised visitor to the set: "Barbra had on a skimpy costume and was very embarrassed when she saw me. I'm really shocked at all these things an actress has to do today... but I guess it's part of the job."

For the first time Barbra Streisand was to undress for the cameras, but even the actress' estranged husband told reporters that she was far too shy to disrobe for the picture. She did balk on the day of filming, although the director had assumed that her fears were long since resolved. The vision of her own nudity clashed with her "nice Jewish girl" upbringing, but she had finally relented for the sake of the role; Ross wondered what was still disturbing her about the crucial scene, and she whispered, "Herbie, I can't. I've got goosebumps and they'll show. Herbie, I just can't. What will my mother think?"

When the director insisted the sexual element was appropriate to such a story, she protested, "Yeah, but I don't think I have that great of a body, and my mother will be unhappy... I don't think I'm ready for it." Although Ross tried to ensure her she would look great, the reluctant woman pulled him into a closet to demonstrate what she feared were her shortcomings. After an hour of procrastination he finally reassured her, adding that the scene would not take long to film; she exclaimed, "Oh, what the hell, I'll do it once." All hands laughed in surprise when she wanted to repeat what the director considered a perfect take. [4-26-70 *L.A. Times*]

Ross noted later: "What will be different about this movie is that you may see Barbra in the nude. At the moment she's a little torn about the decision. She has beautiful bosoms and her vanity wants to show them off. On the other hand, she's still a little intimidated by the whole idea. However, knowing women, I think vanity will win." [11-12-69 *HWD. Reporter*] In the end, vanity lost when Streisand insisted the daring bare breasts would be unacceptable to her family, the actress exercising her privilege of having the five seconds of exposure fogged.

Stark and Ross implored the star to allow the scene to be included in its entirety, but she adamantly refused, insisting that the nudity "spoils the comedy of the next scene," meaning that the rather jarring glimpse of the character's body was too literal for the lightweight movie. She would only be seen in silhouette, and inevitably, the aborted topless scenario was lampooned in the press as a mere publicity stunt. A decade later the men's magazine *High Society* unmasked the actress by unearthing the semi-nude pictures for publication, her subsequent litigation being only partially successful as several hundred of the instant collector's item had already been leaked.

When *The Owl and the Pussycat* script altered its focus from being a realistic comedy to a sentimental melodrama, an anguished Doris was expected to implore Felix to marry her. The actress must have resisted so radical a change, as she found it hard to express the emotion. The weather on the day of the filming had been forecast as bright and clear, but it was cloudy and cold in Central Park, with charcoal heaters provided for the crew but not for the stars. Streisand told Ross she could not cry and she also resisted the fakery of glycerine, but the director reportedly tricked the actress into tears by reminding how fatigued she would be at that evening's *Dolly!* opening after all the filming delays. When Felix forces her to beg like a dog, she complies, then begins crying, until the frustrated woman finally strikes him. Eager for the performing exercise as an animal, the actress in Streisand had originally encouraged the screenwriter to develop the groveling scene. In the end critics would resist this hard-edged finish to the soft-touched comedy.

Production was completed on January 19, 1970, the "exhausted" actress beginning her well-deserved working hiatus which postponed the Riviera commitment in Las Vegas until that autumn. The final scene from *Owl* was reportedly re-shot more than a month later, when a spring weather setting was deemed necessary after all. Streisand then returned briefly to Los Angeles to record a Bergman-Legrand album and for a sneak preview of *On a Clear Day*. As summer approached, the Riviera Hotel was eager for the singer to complete her Vegas engagement, but she told reporters that it was her vacation and that she was only interested in sun, tennis lessons and French language instruction.

In early July the actress privately screened *The Owl and the Pussycat*, which had been trimmed to a snappy running time of 96 minutes. Later in the month she flew from Los Angeles to New York with Jason, vacationing in East Hampton where her son stayed for the summer with his father two blocks from Streisand's rented home. Elliott Gould invited his separated wife to visit him in Sweden to observe the filming of *The Touch*, and she went accompanied by two bodyguards, airfare provided by the actor.

Los Angeles critics were wined and dined before viewing *The Owl and the Pussycat* sneak preview with a paying audience on a midweek night in Westwood, the film-makers hoping that the jaded reviewers would succumb to the enthusiasm of the public viewing the comedy. Stark reversed what he had initially assumed was a liability into a box office plus, promoting, by necessity, Barbra Streisand's first non-musical.

Opening in late November 1970, *The Owl and the Pussycat* became one of the next year's most successful films, 1971's most profitable comedy, Columbia's biggest holiday feature ever. The "sleeper" grossed $12 million its first twelve months and possibly spared the actress an embarrassing letdown of her film career after her sluggish second and third musicals. Certainly broadening her image and appeal, the success proved that the actress was bankable and that *Funny Girl* was not a onetime fluke. For the first time the actress was placed in the Top Ten box office list, Elizabeth Taylor the only woman ranking higher. Streisand's three musicals had been vastly more expensive to create than the modestly-priced comedy which easily multiplied its investment. With her most profitable movies being Rastar Productions, Columbia Pictures earnestly sought another commitment from the actress who instead signed Warners contracts for her next two films.

With its lifelike obscenity and candid scenario, the Streisand comedy was one of the new decade's pivotal pictures marking a turning point in Hollywood. The promotion for the comedy was openly sexual, emphasizing the ribald nature of the adult feature. The print promotion not-so-delicately trumpeted Doris' profession: "When she mixes business with pleasure, she goes out of business." Some editors balked at the hooker's suggestive costume, but even the censored ads proclaimed, "Barbra's broadening the base of her operations." Radio spots blared the simple yet suggestive notion that "*The Owl and the Pussycat* answers the age-old question: `CAN an owl and a pussycat... and if so, HOW?'" Another catchy and provocative scheme: "'The Owl and the Pussycat' is no longer a tale for children..."

*The Owl and the Pussycat* title listed the male character first, but discounting the gossip that he was unhappy not to share the movie advertising with Streisand, Segal realized that it was the star's picture, nor did he want to interfere in their close relationship. They did not compete with each other, possibly because he declined to try, even though she had seemed disinterested in upstaging anyone, the actor said.

The mature romance would allow for some of Streisand's and Segal's best acting performances. Nominated for a Golden Globe in January 1971, her failure to be so recognized by the Motion Picture Academy was mystifying. Streisand unfairly missed what should have been a well-deserved acknowledgment, perhaps an early rejection of an upstart actress, but possibly the material was also too volatile, the comedy's restricted rating an uncharacteristic category for the Streisand of the time. Prostitute roles have long been honored by the voters, but apparently a comic, graphic depiction with its four-letter vocabulary was seen as less than respectable for the lofty institution. The 1973 re-release would be PG-rated, fans protesting the needless culling of "those two words," knowing that Doris' language was appropriate and even necessary for the low-class prostitute. The graphic dialogue kept the comedy from being telecast until 1975, when it was mutilated almost beyond recognition, although an intact version is fortunately available on videocassettes.

It is a rare treat for aficionados, collectors and scholars that the film-makers decided to release on the CBS masterworks label an original soundtrack album which was for years a rare recording, although now reissued for "discriminating listeners." Periodic bursts of "Blood, Sweat and Tears" music from the score were interwoven with selected dialogue.

*The Owl and the Pussycat* featured what was becoming a Streisand staple: roles were reversed, Doris the passionate seducer, the man shy and reluctant. The hilarious plot was related to 1930's and 40's madcap comedies but seemed more rooted in reality. When Felix complains to the landlord that his neighbor is entertaining men for profit, she is evicted. Doris awakens him at 3:00 a.m. and forces her way into the "fruitcake's" apartment. Allowed to stay but only for the night, Doris cannot sleep without a television blaring. Her barging into his room embarrasses the half-undressed prig, and Doris laughs so hard at his modesty that she suffers unrelenting hiccups; his cure is to scare her with his Halloween skeleton costume, but the resulting commotion has both of them ejected in the middle of the night.

They stay at a friend's apartment where another fight is initiated. When he attempted to lull her into a sleep with one of his stories, Doris criticizes his pretentious imagery, such as "the sun spit morning." This intimacy culminates in lovemaking, Felix clumsy and fumbling, the skilled professional orchestrating their actions very enthusiastically-- "Attaboy, attaboy,

attaboy!" Doris is amazed that Felix would have considered himself a "pansy," thinking she had saved him by her skills, even though he tries to explain he never thought of himself as gay. Later, Felix questions Doris about her experienced past and belittles her bedside prowess, which upsets the woman. She condemns his writing, but he dismisses the opinions of a streetwalker. In a fury Doris finally leaves the borrowed apartment, but when he later sees the theater where the porno flick *Cycle Sluts* is playing, he accepts that he actually cares for this Doris Wilgus.

The woman improves her vocabulary in hopes of impressing the intellectual man she desires. Reunited by a friend, they visit Felix' rich fiancée's mansion, which makes Doris jealous, but she decides to bathe her prey when he seems ill. She undresses and climbs in the bathtub with him, introducing the man to the pleasures of smoking pot. The scene culminates with his fiancée returning with her parents, Doris realizing the father is one of her kinky customers. The ending occurs in Central Park, where the unlikely lovers publicly conduct their most vehement verbal scuffle. But he finally makes her accept herself as she is, a hooker, yes, but a reformed edition who sacrifices her false pursuit of easy money. Doris' dignity is left intact. He pretends to meet her for the first time, introducing himself as a bookstore clerk who abandons writing for which he had no real talent. Their pretensions unmasked, they are free to appreciate their true selves and begin anew.

Critics praised the small-scale film which allowed the actress to be herself without having to compete with a dominating oversize production. The two-sided Streisand characterization of overpowering self-assurance one minute, followed by the gentle innocence and defenselessness in the next frame, was a brilliant tour de force. The actress' performance was comic, energized, flamboyant, zany, aggressive, earthy, bawdy, touching, occasionally delicate and vulnerable-- but she was not nominated for an Oscar.

An interesting critical comment was that *The Owl and the Pussycat* should not have become serious toward the end, emphasizing messages about loneliness and looking for solace in others. Reviewers appreciated that the well-known Streisand mannerisms were exploited sensibly for comic effect, but a handful of voices argued that she was too basically talented a performer to play a non-talented actress, the only rebuttal being that it takes talent to portray a no-talent-- a no-talent could not play a no-talent. Many others were delirious in praising the perfect chemistry between the stars who offset each other so well. Critics were impressed with the woman's unabashedly uninhibited and dynamo performance.

January 1970 *Newsweek* cover story journalist Joseph Morganstern had quipped, "It's not a musical, though she hums a bit." Morte Goode, *Time*: "Appearing in her first non-musical, Barbra does not sing a note, but her feline yowling is pure musical comedy." [11-16-70] Vincent Canby in the *New York Times*: "... even though she never sings, it's possible to remember what happens when she does: through the force of a mysterious, implacable talent, she goes a long way toward making one agree that she is-- as she proclaimed in *Funny Girl*-- the greatest star." [11-4-70]

*Mad* magazine "deflated" *The Foul and the Prissy Cat* in a parody, joking that when "Dooris" contracts hiccups, she asks her new friend to scare her, so he holds a mirror before her... She tells him, "I sleep sitting up! Do you think that's strange?" He answers, "No! The audience has been doing it since the movie started!" [9-71]

# Chapter 12

"Barbra Streisand Makes History,

Lives in Las Vegas"

Barbra Streisand's superstar Las Vegas cabaret concerts were in mid-summer 1969, early winter 1970 and the 1971-72 holiday season. Although the singer had been committed since 1963 to perform at the Riviera Hotel, six years later she asked the management to delay her outstanding engagement so she could accept a $1 million offer from the brand-new Hilton International, a salary to be paid over five years averaging $100,000 per week of performing. The cabaret triumph closed a circle, returning to the speakeasy performance which had begun her career. The singer had been persuaded to appear in Las Vegas to facilitate her modern musical transition, told that she needed the exposure before a live audience and opting for a limited Nevada undertaking over a complicated concert tour.

Her contract included an escalating salary of nearly $250,000 per week for return engagements, although the star and the hotel agreed not to discuss the fiscal details. The stellar attraction more than justified the unprecedented salary as a guaranteed lure for the casinos, Barbra Streisand drawing $15 per person plus drinks in the gigantic showroom seating 3,400 for a total of two performances nightly, the vast capacity including balcony bleachers. Rumors of the secretive but widely-speculated financial transaction had ranged from $400,000 to a million, *Variety* calling the long-term commitment "the highest sum ever paid a performer for cafe appearances."

Having built the world's most mammoth resort hotel, the International's owner sought top performers for the crucial opening season that summer. Other acts had rejected the immense showroom until Barbra Streisand finally agreed to debut the grandest of the grand hotels. Manager Marty Erlichman has explained that Streisand embraced the Vegas commitment not for the money but for the excitement aroused in her career in general. The inducement to major stars was the $5 hotel stock offering which Streisand eagerly accepted. It was stipulated that she could buy dividends at then inexpensive prices, 20,000 shares worth $5 each and quickly escalating to $60 a share, later $70, an investment of $100,000 parlayed into $1,200,000 certainly being a sound Vegas gamble.

Having contemplated the contract for six months before signing, Streisand would soon live to regret her decision. Although Erlichman and his only client had been persuaded to inaugurate the Showroom Internationale because of the groundbreaking first, the singer's anxiety was worsened by the incomplete building in which she was expected to rehearse. The prolonged shooting schedule of *On a Clear Day You Can See Forever* had interfered with the performer's preparation for Vegas; she was able to arrive only one week early in the desert capital, where she rented Betty Grable's home.

Wishing the money had gone to starving children instead, she protested when fans lavished costly floral arrangements for her dressing room. Only days before the opening, she found the showroom unfinished, vacant of furniture and the stage totally bare, forcing her to rehearse in an empty room. The manager wanted the singer to become familiar with the other Vegas acts, so they attended various shows. When a "kibitzer" was ejected by security guards at a Dean Martin performance, the insecure performer wondered what kind of heckling she would have to endure. "If they do that to him, what will they do to me?" [10-4-69 *Billboard*] Erlichman threatened to cancel the opening when the hotel's publicists told uninvited members of the press that the star had blacklisted them; in reality she had added nearly twenty names to the suggested list, deleting none of the others.

Streisand was terrified about the rather novel experience of appearing live after the many years in Hollywood and recording studios, having learned to depend upon the comfortable "privacy of the camera," as she phrased it. "By now, I'm totally used to the cocoon-like world of movie-making," but she also desired the live performance to prove she was "not tied to one medium." The International was the largest stage she had ever confronted, causing the most frightening moments of her career.

According to Albert Goldman's controversial *Elvis* biography, the late Presley was himself very reluctant to return to live performing in Vegas that year, having been kept exclusively a studio artist by the manager, "Colonel" Tom Parker. Reportedly, Parker balked at his breadwinner's risking the hazardous debut: "Let somebody else stick his neck out." The author's analysis is that the "ignorant of Vegas" Streisand, overconfident of her fame while also handicapped by the ever-present discomfort with being onstage, "...came to town with an audaciously simple show... It was a stunning exhibition of vocal and stylistic virtuosity by the Heifetz of pop song". It would have been an appropriate smash in the east but despite a celebrity premiere played to not-quite-capacity houses, the widely-heralded opening not totally sustaining the anticipation. Because the recent Oscar-winner could not have been more famous, the expectations for her solo Vegas debut were unrealistic, even to the thought that she might elevate the showroom genre to a more serious kind of performance.

Goldman's selective research failed to note the audience-planning glitch of the hotel's inability to accommodate guests as scheduled, with reservations transferred to the owner's other hotel, the Flamingo. The non-readiness of the new high-rise included empty cigarette urns, wet paint, insufficient air conditioning, a leaky second floor pool which ran into the showroom and poor sound quality which plagued the early shows. Some reviews would be nasty, often not about the performer but about the formal, ostentatious showroom and the undistinguished cuisine.

During the unadorned concert with the stage still bare except for the lavishly-dressed singer and a jeweled microphone, the singer delivered a repertoire similar to her 1967 Central Park format but playing her act straight, with little comedy or dancing. No dancers supported the singer, no warm-up entertainer, no special effects, no costume changes, no elaborate coiffure, her pale straw-colored hair simply flowing straight. Opening on a Wednesday, July 2, 1969, exactly six years after her July 2, 1963 Riviera debut, she performed until the end of the month during a pivotal period of history in which man first walked on the moon.

The singer had anticipated an admitted gamble of running onstage in jeans, shocking the audience used to sophisticated stars but announcing with a characteristic shrug, "The hotel isn't ready yet, either." While the orchestra would play the five-minute overture, she wanted to disappear backstage and return dressed in an elegant gown. She had talked to Gould about the notion finally rejected when she suspected that the crowd would be restless from the heat and other problems with the building, the discomfort especially aggravated by the crowded showroom and the shortage of seats. Ironically, such humor would have lessened the charges from the press of being stiff and aloof.

It was said that the perfectionist singer was disturbed to discover before the opening-night curtain that the Plexiglas runways were dirty, cleaning them herself with Windex and paper towels. Rita Hayworth, the star's idol as a youth, was one of the many celebrities present, but Streisand was afraid of introducing the numerous glitterati in the audience lest she unintentionally offend those she might overlook. Because the first night was such an event, she performed only once.

Opening sardonically with "I Got Plenty of Nuthin,'" she mocked the image of being the world's highest-paid performer. In her own mind the notorious salary only worsened her tension, knowing she was even more on display. She quipped about her raspberry chiffon gown, "This was my bedspread. I just thought I'd put it on and make a costume!" No response. "Welcome to the almost-ready International Hotel. This place is going to look terrific someday-- just shows you what some people can do with a G.I. loan," she kept joking.

The material was quite varied, the 27-year-old not having performed her standards in several years. "Here is a nice song for a hot summer night," she described "Jingle Bells," at the finish catching some of the white stuff coincidentally cascading from the ceiling: "It isn't snow-- it isn't popcorn-- it isn't corn-flakes..." She raised her eyes and exclaimed, "My God, it's plaster!"

After singing songs from *Funny Girl*, Streisand added, "That's from one of my movies. I've made three, but only one has been released. The others are, as they say in the trade, in the can-- which isn't a very good way to say where your movies are." She revealed the plots of *Hello, Dolly!* and *On a Clear Day You Can See Forever* before singing a few highlights from each score. Her contemporary additions were several songs from her upcoming *What About Toady?* album, introducing "Punky's Dilemma" with a sly innuendo, "Now here's a song from the guy who really made Mrs. Robinson-- Paul Simon, of Simon and Garfunkel."

With her 18 songs and the 37-member house orchestra (providing her own musical conductor, Peter Matz), it was indeed a concert and not a typical speakeasy act. The singer disdained the casual, comic camaraderie with the boozy spectators and simply performed, although intensely, such clean professionalism being attacked as remote and routine, even the audience demanding an intimacy from her.

A New York reviewer's ironic pronouncement was that the show was "over rehearsed." Conservative critics judged "Jingle Bells" in July as gimmicky and protested the torch rendition of "Punky's Dilemma." Early reports complained that the star was cold, scarcely uttering an extra word with her perfunctory performance. The press challenged the over-dressed and mechanical woman's obvious nervousness, the introduction of new material from her current album, the pro-motion of her three films, and especially the "self-conscious banter," her scripted patter deemed less inspired than her own adlibbed humor.

Some reports indicate that the singer sang too much, in the sense of not establishing rapport with the audience by talking very warmly to them between numbers. A sharp indictment from Michael Etchison of the *L.A. Herald Examiner*: "All Barbra Streisand did was sing. Clearly, she was using the songs as a medium for Streisand, and not the other way around. And Streisand had nothing to say." [7-4-69]

*Hollywood Reporter*:

> "Barbra Streisand is very fortunate indeed to be making a reputed $100,000 a week at the posh new International. Now she can afford to get someone to write an act for her. It would be money well spent. Her voice, a remarkable instrument about which enough has been said . . . comes through fine. But never does she warm to the people or they to her. The sameness of arrangements, the sameness of the treatment she gives each song, makes for such monotony you can't believe. A real `live' Barbie doll."

The concluding paragraph could not have been more snide: "There was no standing ovation." [7-9-69]

The morning after the opening, the singer acknowledged her qualms and the uncomfortable distance. "I don't enjoy working in front of a bunch of strangers." The 55-minute performance managed to withstand the hostile critics, and with further refinement the engagement closed even more successfully than it had begun. Hurt by the initial reception, she had altered the act and was gratified to find the crowds reacting more favorably. She felt that the problem had been her overreaction to the size of the crowd by trying too hard. The performer considered it an anachronism for her actual antiestablishment character to be showcased in the traditional café arena where she was expected to shine with sophistication and glamour, singing only her greatest hits. · Her unhappiness naturally detracted from the ease of performing she had demonstrated at her two outdoor concerts only two years prior, and as with *Funny Girl* on Broadway, she X'ed the remaining days from her dressing-room calendar.

In a revealing backstage interview, Streisand complained to *L.A. Times* editor Charles Champlin that his review had not analyzed why she was distant on her opening night. The writer had noted that the "cool aloofness" was worsened by a performance which was "too talky," but he would come to appreciate that the jubilant closing had displayed less prepared talk, the remaining chatter being crisp and sardonic, friendly and confident. In response, the singer explained how traumatic it had been to rediscover her fears of the audience, an emotion acquired during *Funny Girl* on Broadway. "I'd hear myself doing the lines or singing but it was like hearing a stranger. It drove me into analysis."

Facing a cabaret audience after six years, she was simply scared. "I was aloof on opening night because I was in a state of shock. You could feel the hostility of that opening night audience, all the gamblers who were there because they're important to the hotel, all the actors who resent the fact that you're doing things they think they should be doing." It was not rewarding to sing to so many unknown people in the audience. Elvis Presley told her he was especially charged by the challenge of warming up a negative audience, but for her it was the opposite reaction, actually obscene and exhibitionistic. [8-5-69 *L.A. Times*]

She was determined to be a smash in Vegas, and her engagement would end with standing ovations, the hordes of fans steadily growing into historical numbers. Although still infrequently, she was eventually able to banter comfortably with the audience. One night she pointed to the casino and joked, "They want you high-rollers in there!" She confided at another point, "I really like this place. It's so nutty. There are no clocks anywhere, no Bibles. Some rooms have them but they only have five commandments."

When first exposed to the unique gambling center in 1963 she had been fascinated, especially with the scarcity of clocks: "Time stood still." She sometimes had a novel audience: big losers too pensive really to hear her performance. She gambled in the casino, playing blackjack with $2 bets, neither really winning nor losing. As a guest dealer she was also tipped $12 by two tourists.

One of Streisand's performances was videotaped onstage at great cost and trouble. The show intended to be more personal and private than the spacious open-air Central Park Happening concert had been and was supposedly scheduled for a CBS one-woman special. Streisand owned the footage and retained the right to release or not, possibly the troubled opening precluding her agreement to broadcast. Showman Ed Sullivan taped another Streisand recital during the second week. *Dolly!* and *Clear Day* samplings opened his first show in the 1969-1970 season, which may have been all the singer intended as a means of promoting her film musicals. She taped *The Ed Sullivan* special before a late-night audience of her peers, the work stretching from 2:30 a.m. until 4:00. She complained, "It's strange when you open your mouth and nothing comes out. I could sing loud but I couldn't sing soft." [10-4-69 *Billboard*]

As the International's successor, "the King" flew into town after Streisand had been headlining for two weeks. One evening Elvis Presley discreetly attended the show of the only competitor who could match his legend.

He silently motioned to the vacant balcony seats nearby, his reaction to the woman's performance impassive and joyless and with obvious distaste for the Jewish preoccupations. He told one of the paid retinue, "She sucks!", but in her dressing room he pretended to have been appreciative.

Presley was amazed that the woman was unaccompanied; "Elvis had never been alone for one moment in his entire life." Swearing never again to appear in Vegas, Streisand complained about her audience and the International, bitter that the structure was still under construction. "I wouldn't be surprised if some night while I'm out there working some schmuck doesn't walk by with a ladder on his shoulder!" The mistaken judgment of the Presley biographer Albert Goldman is assuming that Streisand's wishing Presley well for his engagement was as genuine as Presley's false compliments.

Priscilla Presley's autobiography *Elvis and Me* related yet another story:

"One night we visited Barbra Streisand backstage at the International Hotel, now the Hilton. It was a classic Streisand performance and Elvis, after a few too many Bloody Marys, wanted to tell Barbra his impressions. We were ushered backstage to her dressing room and Elvis's first words upon meeting her were: `What did you ever see in Elliott Gould? I never could stand him.' In typical Streisandese she retorted, `Whaddya mean? He's the fah-tha of my child!'-- leaving Elvis speechless."

Streisand delayed her final International appearance from midnight until 2:30 a.m. so that her peers could finish their own late-night shows and be able to attend her last performance. At closing night-- the showroom packed just to the fire code's limit with 2,000 people and 200 standees-- she received three standing ovations. A sore throat affecting her vocals strained some high notes. She made an introduction: "I want to introduce someone who is... who is, well, you see him on television and you hear him on records and... [looking up] well, Elvis Presley!" He rose from his seat to bow, and she continued, "Elvis, you will be up here in my place tomorrow night and you'll love it, just as I do. Tonight, and many of the nights here, have been pure joy for me."

Elvis Presley's follow-up engagement was heavily promoted, although the "Colonel" waited until the first possible second on July 29 when Streisand's own time had contractually ended at midnight, when a blitzkrieg of Parker's extreme hype then bombarded the city. Presley was essentially a Vegas artist from this point until his death in 1977.

After Streisand's engagement ended, the innkeeper Alex Shoofey hosted an after-hours party for the big names in town, the guest of honor arriving late with her escort Peter Matz. Shoofey presented the singer with a $6,000 gold watch and six complete tennis outfits personalized with her name on each item. After this rigorous mid-summer historical engagement, Erlichman and Streisand planned for the professional pace to ease in 1970 after the late-year filming of *The Owl and the Pussycat*, expecting to be able to concentrate on recordings once again. She intended to withdraw from work, which she did for nearly a year, not working again until she returned to Vegas in late 1970.

Barbra on the cover of Volume II.

Barbra on the cover of Volume I.

# Chapter 13

"On a Clear Day You Can See Forever
a Musical about Reincarnation?"

After lyricist Alan Jay Lerner's longtime partner Frederick Lowe died, the famous songwriter's next composer was Burton Lane. Their last collaboration was the Broadway score *On a Clear Day Day You Can See Forever*, a solid if not spectacular success totalling 280 performances. It starred Barbara Harris at the same time as *Funny Girl* down the block. The late Alan Jay Lerner's classic *My Fair Lady* theme of the commoner transformed into a regal lady was reincarnated in this latter story.

Paramount Pictures acquired the $750,000 screen rights in the spring of 1966, and producer Howard Koch decided the woman who was clearly the most exciting musical performer in the world would be perfect. The studio negotiated with Barbra Streisand during her London *Funny Girl* engagement, but she declined the project. Koch considered other actresses but was determined to convince the musical superstar, no matter how long and how expensive it might prove to be. Even the songwriters wrote new material exclusively for the performer uniquely suitable for the uncommon role.

Appealing to her well-known need for artistic freedom, the producer finally enticed the actress by offering an unusual advance approval of the creative team. When she was in her last months of pregnancy and inactive professionally, he dangled a generous salary and Streisand finally relented in

January of 1967. After the complicated negotiation, the young actress was signed for what would be her third picture, three major musicals in a row.

The actress' $350,000 salary did not include her lucrative fee from Columbia Records, the company releasing the film soundtrack. Motivated by his *Gigi* jewel, the star's first choice for director was the legendary Vincente Minnelli. She also suggested Harry Stradling as cinematographer, the gifted man who would photograph both *Funny Girl* and *Hello, Dolly!*, and Cecil Beaton as costumer. The actress was allowed to film for Columbia Pictures and 20th Century-Fox first, so the *Clear Day* production was postponed, pre-production set for early October 1968.

Like the other Hollywood studios, Paramount had entered the high-budget musical sweepstakes initiated by the historical success of *The Sound of Music*, their bid for smash box office being the $9 million production of the famous Alan Jay Lerner's newest musical. *OACYCSF* was Streisand's first film which featured a lesser-known theme and score; basically a play with music but few elaborate production numbers, after the opening number no songs are heard for thirty minutes. The film gave the actress what she considered her meatiest role yet, finally enabling her to play a contemporary woman although for only half of the time, since flashback sequences made the musical another period piece.

The story concerned an average, everyday woman who had lived many previous lives, some of which were quite colorful, although the unpretentious film wisely did not take its whimsical premise too seriously. Daisy Gamble at her fiancé's insistence consults a psychoanalyst to kick her smoking habit, when a whole other personality is discovered. From his new patient Yves Montand unearths a past life in England as a titled Regency-era aristocrat, Melinda Winifred Waine-Tentrees. Daisy's Brooklyn Jewish accent is totally absent as Melinda, a two-part role proving that the actress' early ethnicity was a mantle, easily shed or assumed. Technically Streisand was not playing two different roles, reincarnation devotees well aware that she was playing the same character removed by hundreds of years.

The actress relished the dual characterizations because it suited what she called her "schizophrenic personality," referring to the polarity of a timid girl alongside the tough woman. Regarding Daisy as a street urchin and Melinda as a seductress, the actress described herself, "I am a cross between a washerwoman and a princess. I am a bit coarse, a bit low, a bit vulgar, and a bit ignorant. But I am also partly princess--sophisticated, elegant, and controlled. I can appeal to everyone." [*Life*]

*On a Clear Day* was a G-rated escapist fantasy with which the audiences could identify, easily imagining exciting previous lives. Hoping to incorporate the growing public consciousness in reincarnation, the studio moguls intended to widen the popular appeal of the story. Years before a young Irish woman Bridey Murphy had stirred quite a tempest with her revelation of past lives, specific details which were proven historically accurate. Teresa Wright and Louis Hayward had starred in the 1956 black-and-white drama *The Search for Bridey Murphy*, which may have been the original inspiration for the 1960's *Clear Day* stage musical.

The career of Vincente Minnelli was rather inactive. He had not not directed a film in five years, or a musical since the Academy Award-winning *Gigi* in 1958, and the film musical pioneer was irresistibly drawn to a Streisand production. The late director clearly marked the film with his singular, lavish style. His autobiography *I Remember It Well* noted his certainty of exceeding the promise of the modest Broadway success with a beautiful visual translation onscreen. He especially mesmerized the audience with attractive flashback sequences.

Seven original Broadway songs were retained. The title number was sung twice, once as an introduction about a very different person named Daisy and reprised at the end with the theme of accepting oneself as well as colorfully envisioning the future. New material was written expressly for the actress-singer: "Love with All the Trimmings," "Go to Sleep" and "E.S.P.". The latter was a fascinating production number in which Daisy would appear as all her previous lives, singing in a montage of five languages, French, Italian, Spanish, German and English. One week alone was allocated to filming the scene which no doubt would have elicited an appreciative response from the audiences but which was regrettably cut.

Arnold Scaasi fashioned the contemporary costumes, Cecil Beaton the elegant period versions, to her joy, although the two designers created clothes with perhaps too much contrast for the different eras. Streisand was actually surprised that the studio deemed it necessary to originate expensive and elaborate costumes when quite suitable gowns were already available. When performing in Vegas in autumn 1970, she told the audience, "The period clothes cost a fortune. I tried talking to them, why not pick up the things at a thrift shop? Save all that money, ya know-- they didn't listen."

Cecil Beaton remembered the star's unusual idea for the glamorous Regency Period shooting: "She wanted to wear a diamond in her nose, and she came to the set with it on. However, it was vetoed. I admired her very much for having wanted it." [5-70 *Movie News*] Beaton said that he was never worried about "going too far" with the woman, whom he found to be fearless of new ideas and challenges. She had to be completely convinced of an idea's validity before she would accept it. "She'll never just say, `Oh, I suppose that's all right, let's go out to dinner.' It's a constant battle of attrition with her and her taste-- which is very exhausting." [12-16-69 *Look*]

As a photographer Beaton had already made contact with Streisand earlier in her career, and as a costumer he genuinely esteemed the woman who was startlingly young but so aware of herself and the film as a whole. He appreciated working with a thoughtful actress, instead of his having to provide all the ideas. They thoroughly analyzed their project, and he thrived with the challenge of satisfying a difficult-to-please artist who matched his own demanding perfectionism.

For the biography *Streisand Through the Lens*, Hollywood journalist George Hadley-Garcia interviewed the acclaimed costumer and photographer just before his 1980 death. "I recall one of the reviewers found the Streisand performance as an English aristocrat reminiscent of vintage Joan Greenwood.

I enjoyed reading that, because both women display a quality of cunning refinement. Barbra did an English accent to perfection; perhaps in an earlier life she was a landed lady with titles and royal lovers. It is a pity Barbra doesn't do more period material. She is an ideal mannequin and a compelling actress in elegant period costumes. Her face is a painting from several historical eras. Barbra as an Englishwoman, an Egyptian, or a Ming empress would be unforgettable." The costumer hid these "historical features" with the turban, which they had both suggested independent of the other. "Barbra has a less monotonously American-type [look] than most actresses of her nationality."

Reportedly, Arnold Scaasi had refused at one time to consider the young offbeat Barbra Streisand as a client, telling her she was not a "Scaasi Girl," but later he was happy to work with the developing sophisticate. The designer flew to the west coast from New York to discuss the picture's contemporary fashions, and when he had tried to leave for a dinner appointment after a full day's session, he was not offended by the actress' question, "Arnold, why did you come to Los Angeles?" He realized that his purpose was to work and not socialize, so he cancelled his engagement and they worked on Daisy's designs until midnight.

The film-makers decided that a French actor would create the kind of memorable casting chemistry they were seeking, and Yves Montand was announced as Barbra Streisand's co-star. Vincente Minnelli readily accepted the unusual pairing of the Jewish actress and the French actor as true to the story of unlikely lovers. When Montand first met the "incomparable" Streisand, he was quite complimentary and charming. "She has that special magic that very few performers generate and I find her a total professional, a perfectionist both for herself and her fellow performers... and an enchantingly feminine woman to boot."

After the *Funny Girl* premieres and with *Hello, Dolly!* finished, the actress began working full-time at her third film studio. Beginning in early October 1968 on the Paramount lot, where the star undertook makeup and costume tests as well as consulted with the producer about the script, the actors rehearsed the involved musical for a total of eight weeks. Half the score was pre-recorded, the other half scheduled to be recorded live during the filming.

The pressure to finalize the picture only inspired the creative actress, and as Howard Koch characterized their relationship, "Working with Barbra Streisand is like making love. She'll know twenty different ways of doing a scene, and it's so much fun finding the right way." She seemed to agree, later telling a reporter that compromising between her personal ideas and those of the film-makers actually spurred her enthusiasm: "I like the challenge of working under battle conditions." The actress was lucky to be on the set by 10:00 in the morning: "I'm very thrilled like when I'm on time." Something always caused a delay, she explained. [12-69 *Look*]

The famous publicity photograph of Streisand and Montand with the studio's other stars had not been planned. Sitting and talking on the steps of the writers' building, the *Clear Day* co-stars were joined in succession by Lee Marvin and Alan Jay Lerner, studio moguls Bernie Donnenfeld and Robert Evans, John Wayne, Clint Eastwood and Rock Hudson. With the stars gathered, it was then an inspired suggestion to summon a photographer. Adolph Zukor, the 96-year-old founder of Paramount Studios, also visited Streisand on the set.

Koch and Lerner hosted a social event of the season, the *Clear Day* production's famous Reincarnation Ball, in which a large group of celebrities was invited to attend costumed as "anybody in world history you might like to have been in a previous lifetime." Hollywood's important stars graced the January 3, 1969 function at the Beverly Hilton Hotel, five hundred renowned but disguised guests celebrating the start of filming. Hoping to boost future box office, the unusual theme of the party naturally garnered the studio international advance publicity.

Principal photography began three days after the costume ball, the six-month production due to finish on the tenth of May. An 82-day shooting was originally planned, including eight or nine location days in England and two days in New York City. Soon after filming began, Streisand was committed to leave for a little over a week to attend the French and British *Funny Girl* premieres. Her absence was inconvenient, but further success of the actress' first film would only increase the chances of *Clear Day*'s box office, and so Minnelli shot around the star for ten days.

By this film, the young performer's confidence had grown, and the cast and crew were more accepting of her perfectionism, her behavior considered especially appropriate to the sole female superstar. Like William Wyler, Minnelli refrained from overdirecting the actress, specifically intending to be harmonious partners with her and not a dictator. The director preferred to supervise his actors as they determined their own characterizations. Streisand was still given to numerous late-night calls about her performance, although the director preferred to leave his work at the studio.

Trusting her first instincts, Streisand had instantly liked Vincente Minnelli, especially when he did not flaunt his legendary successes or belittle her novice career. "He's so open and trusts my instincts so. I guess he must have liked my work or something." The director welcomed many of her suggestions and was happy to make the changes. He enjoyed their endless conversations, although he gently encouraged her not to call him at home. Minnelli said she generally accepted his advice, especially if he explained himself well. Although he has noted that she declined to discuss the schizophrenic characterization with a psychiatrist, as he had proposed, we know she had seen an analyst since the Broadway *Funny Girl*. The director encouraged the brilliant cinematographer's capturing the unique Streisand beauty without changing her appearance.

When the producer interviewed the then-unknown actor Jack Nicholson (*Easy Rider* not yet released) for the small role as Daisy's ex-stepbrother, Koch introduced him to Streisand, believing in the importance of cordial relations with the show's star before committing supporting players. The producer was delighted that she volunteered to help Nicholson with what was for him an unanticipated reading of the role with Minnelli, who had seen Nicholson in *Psych-Out*. Apparently the original plot would have allowed Daisy to accept the true love she felt for Tad Pringle, the unexplained last-minute alterations causing confusion for the audiences.

The actor was never asked if he could sing for the musical, his one attempt later dropped. Jack Nicholson has always characterized his inadequate role as having been one which he accepted basically for the money. The actor considered his presence to be the producers' hopes of broadening the appeal to younger audiences; he recognized that Daisy's ex-stepbrother was a tangent to the story, merely added gratuitously and later cut severely. With the eventual male superstar as her duet partner, Streisand added a very low flute-like humming to match his vocals, the scene filmed on Daisy's rooftop terrace. He has explained, "Barbra, when we actually started shooting my song, decided she would like to sing (actually, hum) on the tail end of the song with me instead of making it a solo. Streisand treated me great, man. I don't think she saw *Easy Rider* either, so it wasn't because of that. She tried to help in my scenes, you know?"

Budget complications evidently cancelled the five-day shooting of the promising production number in which Daisy appears as all of her previous incarnations. Perhaps the overlong film precluded the complicated "E.S.P." footage. The actress worried about explaining to the film-makers that she preferred to sing the musical's love song alone on the sound-stage, having to fantasize to whom she was singing. She refused to divulge the unknown identity, although the producer continued to query her in later years.

The Goulds had separated a month after filming began, although the actor was still staying with his estranged wife while he filmed *Bob & Carol & Ted & Alice*. He agreed to escort her to the Academy Awards. When the actress reported for work on the *Clear Day* set after winning the *Funny Girl* Oscar the prior night, she was surprised that the cast and crew honored her with a congratulatory party. Signs were carried: "Daisy, we knew you'd win!" and "We love you..."

Three or four days after the actress won the esteemed accolade from her peers, the studio flew the cast and a reduced crew to New York City for outdoor filming. On the eastbound TWA flight the producers surprised the actress with a party in the air, her 27th birthday on April 24, 1969, with all 25 passenger-guests enjoying the food and champagne. The east coast location scenes were at the Oak Room of the Plaza Hotel as well as the Central Park Zoo where the strangely-dressed Daisy appears as a character from her future life. The public complicated the filming by swarming along the sidewalks. Streisand was paid $50 a day for using her own Thunderbird car for a scene, as well as $50 for the scene with her dog. Sadie was earning her keep, her owner quipped.

The company next flew to London for the Regency sequences, filming in England for two costly weeks. The elegant hippie arrived in London dressed in furs and bell-bottoms and indulged in some enjoyable antiquing expeditions while overseas, accompanied by his son, Jason. Australian actor George Lazenby met Streisand in Britain, and the young pair enjoyed several outings.

The early eighteenth-century Regency Period depicted the character's aristocratic background, Streisand cultivating an upper-crust British accent by talking with actress Deborah Kerr. "Wouldn't it be great if the whole Brooklyn thing was a put-on?", she asked rhetorically. Like Cecil Beaton, Minnelli also admitted his surprise that the actress devised her own rich British accent, summoning the voice from a seemingly endless source of talent.

The overseas filming was highlighted by the Brighton Pavilion scenes, a location considerably cheaper than creating a reproduction in Hollywood. Streisand described the gaudy excess of the famous Royal Pavilion, "It's a combination of the grotesque and the beautiful. And it's grotesquely beautiful." Critics would praise the exquisite circling close-ups of the actress during the giant ballroom's seduction scene with John Richardson. It would also be observed that another glorious WASP succumbed to the legendary Jewess. The actress influenced the glamorous banquet costume, the white jeweled turban and matching lowcut crepe gown, with strands of pearls hanging down her forehead.

The company returned to New York in mid-May, when subsequent location shooting days were added. Streisand also accepted a Friars Club Entertainer of the Year tribute at this time. Unable as anticipated to create the demonstration scenes at Fordham University in New York City, the studio decided to postpone the campus filming until summer when the students were absent, fearful of the tense political environment. Columbia University too declined the filming, having already been plagued by a genuine student eruption. In the end the University of Southern California doubled for the brief campus activity.

The college complications meant that the film went into hiatus, the actress' contract expiring on May 21. Believing they had a blockbuster film in the works, none of the film-makers objected to the schedule's being delayed several weeks. But the production had had a guaranteed completion date for the performer to rest and prepare for her important Vegas engagement upcoming in July. The situation was widely debated in Hollywood, with *Variety* predicting that Streisand had the upper hand with the studio being forced to capitulate to her demands, but of course the actress would not have imperiled her own picture.

In lieu of additional salary, she requested a trailer, which the studio officials thought was odd, including wardrobe and windows, all of which were estimated to be worth $75,000. The renewed contract allowed her to choose certain furnishings from the sets, and it gave the woman a kick to have her offer accepted to work half-a-day without pay in exchange for the beveled leaded Victorian glass panels she prized. Ironically, the actress might have been given the props as a parting gift anyway, Koch later noted. Further irony was that the campus episode lasted only fleeting seconds on the screen when the picture was slashed.

Streisand gave Minnelli an antique silver coffee service inscribed, "To Vincente whom I adore... Love, Barbra." She had written on the creamer "You're the cream in my coffee." The actress thoughtfully declined to include the sugar bowl, as the director was forbidden the sweet indulgence. She was pleased that when giving her a study of Sarah Bernhardt, he predicted the inevitability of her portraying the French actress someday.

The actress killed hundreds of still pictures, and because of her famed uncertainty she had $25,000 worth of photographs retouched, unusual for any actress, and even those were for the most part finally rejected. Said the film's producer, "She looks at herself pretty rough and emphasizes her good points-- her eyes, her nose, her hands and her beautiful skin. And she's the homeliest gorgeous lady I've ever met." [12-16-69 *Look*]

Four scenes were cut from the 143-minute *On a Clear Day You Can See Forever* print. Fourteen minutes included Nicholson's song with Streisand and the detailed production number. The abbreviated running time was 129 minutes-- long enough, it might seem. It is possible that the original roadshow version will be restored, as successfully occurred in 1983 with the mangled 1954 *A Star Is Born*. The *Clear Day* footage will not be difficult to locate as was Judy Garland's musical scenes.

Released June 17, 1970, six months after *Hello, Dolly!*, *On a Clear Day You Can See Forever* was like the earlier musical, not a smash hit but not a failure either. Both Big Event musicals were intended to attract huge audiences, and the rather average attendance was disappointing. The films drew crowds but not the droves required to recoup the excessive production costs. The problem was simple arithmetic, the budgets so grossly swollen that only historically large audiences would have been profitable.

Paramount Studios was jittery about the commercial prospects of what had originally been its three-hour roadshow property-- a soon-to-be-extinct breed-- and the company distributed the musical in a saturation release. The star was not present at the opening. The studio hoped that the nation's young audiences would flock to the many theaters showing the musical, just to see Barbra Streisand who after the Paramount filming had accepted her second Golden Globe as World Film Favorite.

Although the picture had originally been intended as an autumn roadshow musical, with limited distribution. A blockbuster that summer would have been unlikely when the musical was obscured by the season's youth-oriented films. The studio was nevertheless surprised with the unexpected box office returns. The public continuing to buy tickets throughout the summer, *Clear Day* nearly repaying its investment if not becoming actually lucrative, the $10,000,000 financing finally returned with the foreign distribution and broadcast rights.

Conducted and arranged by the legendary Nelson Riddle, the film score was a Columbia Records release pressed on the Masterworks label. The soundtrack album was released curiously, perhaps complicated by the different studios involved. The score was butchered in a senseless attempt to salvage the box office profits-- and as a result, three soundtrack versions are available, one a Columbia Records "Special Product for discriminating buyers" reissued in later years and the original soundtrack which had not even reached the Top 100 on the charts, dying at #108 as the worst-selling Streisand soundtrack. The third version was the very original demo album, including the cut songs, this extremely rare collector's item including Jack Nicholson's solo "Who is There Among Us Who Knows?" for which Streisand shared her lowest, smoky-voiced humming.

*Clear Day* is the only Streisand musical to have received no Academy Award nominations whatsoever, certainly a crime in technical fields, such as costuming and cinematography. Minnelli defensively noted in his memoirs, "The picture finished shooting on schedule. It was not my greatest musical success, but neither was it Paramount's greatest musical failure." A later analysis: "I can only guess that perhaps the division into a modern story and a period story confused some people or dissatisfied others. And the picture may have been too genteel for its time, with the war and the protests and pictures like *Easy Rider*. I think it's much better appreciated now." [Quoted by George Hadley-Garcia/*Barbra Now & Then* #4]

The actress acknowledged in a December 1970 interview, "*Clear Day* I liked. I liked the concept, but didn't feel it was fulfilled as a movie. But that's beyond my control, and I don't have any control over my movies." A few years later she still lamented, "`Hello, Dolly' and `On a Clear Day' would have made money, except the schmucks at the studio kept pouring more money into them, at a time when big musicals were out.... `Dolly' and `On a Clear Day' were not good pictures." [Jerry Parker interview/late 73 *Newsday*]

Always dissatisfied with the film versions of his musicals, as the executive producer Alan Jay Lerner had obviously hoped to wield more control with *Clear Day*. He has complained that Daisy was overdressed, so that no strong division was created between the two incarnations, and neither were the modern-day counterpart's clothes in keeping with the late sixties' styles. Lerner lost the battle with Minnelli and Streisand that at the ending Daisy should be ignorant of her past lives, leaving the irony intact. The writer also advocated Daisy's being kept unilluminated about the future, Lerner considering it farcical for her to reveal that in the year 2038 they would wed in later lives and then walking away from each other in the present, but he was dissuaded. [*Bright Lights*, Vol. 3, No. 1]

Yves Montand moaned and groaned to reporters that the star was responsible for diminishing his role. "Streisand had the right to cut this film herself, so she cut me out so there could be more of her. Now I just have a supporting role in that film." Years later he was still bitchy and implacably bitter: "It was to have been a more equitable sharing of the movie. That was what I thought. I knew in her own country, she was already the bigger star. But there was very little give. I worked with Monroe, and she knew she was beloved of the public, but she didn't bring it with her on the set. They gave Streisand everything she wanted, and more. It was eventually decided to change it from a movie version of the play, into a picture for her: a Barbra Streisand picture. Even then, the people who adored her did not go and make it into a hit." [Quoted by George Hadley-Garcia/*Barbra Now & Then* #3]

These foolish remarks are an obviously groundless charge: from the beginning, as written, the man's role was always supporting. Even Minnelli later defended the unjust accusation, as he was solely responsible as director for the final cut. He included every scene of the actor's, only cutting Streisand's sequences which were considered overlong, mostly the musical numbers. Even Koch and Lerner years later acknowledged the miscasting of Montand, knowing that little if any chemistry was created and wishing that Richard Harris had accepted the role.

Montand had raved about the actress initially, but he vowed never to do an American film, and has not. If one artist can be blamed for the troubles with the musical, it would be his performance, the actor's English pronunciations atrocious. Critics attacked Montand and accused him of alienating audiences with his readily-apparent disdain for Daisy. Audiences obviously cared little whether he won the woman or not, the particular sexlessness between them especially worsened by their hardly touching or kissing.

The music of *On a Clear Day You Can see Forever* is golden-toned, superior to the book and lyrics. Critics applauded the aura of glamour returned to films after so long, but many others missed the intangible spark which makes a truly great musical. It was agreed that Lerner's screenplay was better than the stageplay but was so badly butchered in editing that the dialogue was baffling. The reincarnation sequences were especially mutilated, too abbreviated to be lucid.

Reviewers hailed Streisand's playing a human being and not a mythical larger-than-life being. *Clear Day* notices were among her most enthusiastic, commentators focusing on the actress' beauty more so than ever before, especially in the gorgeous Old English showcase at the Brighton Pavilion. Not only was a sensitive actress revealed but so too was a bright and impromptu comedienne with faultless timing. Her singing was considered a parody of Joan Greenwood's purring vocals, the sincere British performer known both for her excesses and restraint.

John Simon's most ridiculous Streisand film review was of *Clear Day*, the critic's words being so self-incriminating one needs only a no-comment quotation to damn the critic, but one should remember that he attacked the intelligence of the reader and the public at large:

> What is it about America that takes a repellent, egomaniacal female impersonator-- whose ostensible gift is belting or shrilling out songs, but one whose real one is making love to herself on stage, screen, and TV-- so readily to its collective bosom? I believe that it is a collective inferiority complex, an overwhelming sense of anonymous submersion in an egoless mass society, from which the Great Masturbator sticks out in what appears to be heroic defiance. Outrageousness is confused with courageness; vulgarity becomes the incarnation of the people's dream (let us not forget that the word comes from vulgas, people), and shamelessness the overcoming of our natural national timidity. I also believe that any pro-nounced member of a minority group-- Negro, Jewish, Indian-- who basks in its real or presumed characteristics, captures not only the benevolence of that group but also much guilt-induced applause from the oppressive minority. [*Movies Into Film, Film Criticism*, 1967-1970]

# Chapter 14

"Barbra Streisand's

Early Recording Portfolio"

In 1978 *Barbra Streisand's Greatest Hits, Volume Two* would become the nation's best-selling album, reaching #1 on the *Billboard* charts. The first such compilation was more of a "best of" album than actual chart-topping radio successes, *Greatest Hits, Volume Two* charted only as high as #32 after being released in late 1969. A greatest hits package by the age of twenty-five, the singer's 13th album was a collection of songs from most of the preceding one dozen Columbia LP's.

CBS Records slyly advertised the recording, "Who could turn her down?... You know, Barbra will probably get into all kinds of homes with this album. Even Park Ave. Duplexes," the message alluding to a well-publicized discrimination case against the singer's residing in New York. On the cover the head-and-shoulders pose shows the bare-breasted singer demurely covered with thick strands of a long wig, held with a hand on which she wore even then what looked like her wedding ring.

Despite the full-length version included on this portfolio work, "Sam, You Made the Pants Too Long" had never been an actual album cut, merely a brief part of the medley for *Color Me Barbra*. Two Grammy winners, the sensitive love ballad "People" and the rejuvenated Democratic Party theme song "Happy Days Are Here Again," her two most successful 1960's hits, were featured on *Greatest Hits*, as well as the catchy "Second Hand Rose," an upbeat song which had been included in the poverty songs medley on the *My Name Is Barbra, Two* album. Due to lack of room, the famous Fanny Brice number was not included on the film soundtrack. Streisand has admitted not being fond of the song although surprised by the public's affection for it. It is odd that the moderate hit single "Stout Hearted Men," which she had sung as a slow ballad, was not included.

Another sixties hit, "He Touched Me," came from the short-lived musical play *Drat! The Cat!* starring Elliott Gould and Leslie Ann Warren (before she married Jon Peters). Perhaps Streisand recorded the song to help publicize her husband's musical, which got poor notices, but the ballad nevertheless is one of her best.

# Chapter 15

*"Hello, Dolly!*

Filming a 134-Year-Old Story"

Barbra Streisand's phenomenal public following evident after her film debut in *Funny Girl* disabused the notion that the legendary Hollywood star system had disappeared and that a single name could no longer become bankable. With seemingly unlimited projects handed to her, the Hollywood newcomer finally chose to star in *Hello, Dolly!*, although years later she complained that she had not desired the role. "I tried to talk them out of it. I was driven to it because of all the publicity. I don't regret doing anything, but that's my `almost regret.'" [12-28-72 Earl Wilson column]

The cinema version of *Hello, Dolly!* obviously looked good on paper. Seemingly a guaranteed smash, Streisand's second picture became an embarrassing regret, a bulky carnival-like musical production which heavily obscured the actress' performance. The disappointment was not the problem of the star-- very likely any combination of casting would have still been unable to salvage the elephantine movie, a matter of quantity before quality. The musical was budgeted by Twentieth Century-Fox at $20-25 million, a super-spectacle becoming so huge until it could not support its own weight and which summarily crashed.

*Hello, Dolly!* was a hit per se although not the record box office the studio had assumed; the overwhelmingly astronomical investment was simply too costly for the studio to make a profit.  It was to be the most expensive musical ever produced, and considering the warping effect of inflation, the budget is still incredible.   Only *Cleopatra* had cost more, but the previous picture's escalating expenses had not been anticipated, making *Hello, Dolly!* the highest-budgeted film in history.

In the sense of publicity, the Streisand musical was a media event, genuine history.   The film is immortalized at the Hollywood Wax Museum, in television and cable broadcasting and in video and laserdisc copies.  A failure is a Streisand film that makes no impression, such as *Up the Sandbox* and *All Night Long*.  Whereas a disastrous film like *Heaven's Gate* was blasted by the reviewers, the Streisand less-than-hit films were still critically regarded as important contributions to that year's offerings.   In fact, *Hello, Dolly!* actually made money-- eventually returned its investment-- but it was not *The Sound of Music* blockbuster the studio had taken for granted.  *Hello, Dolly!*'s shelf life has proven amazingly durable, more Hollywood mileage gained from *Dolly!* than from a smash hit, such as, for example, *What's Up, Doc?*

The Broadway musical triumph had opened January 16, 1964, only two months before *Funny Girl* premiered.   The Carol Channing play won nine Tony Awards, the classic sweep precluding its closest competitor-- *Funny Girl*-- from winning any categories.  In early 1965 Twentieth Century-Fox brought the film rights to *Hello, Dolly!* for $2.1 million, with Doris Day, Shirley MacLaine and Julie Andrews then being considered for the title role.

The story was actually well over a century old, and the long history of the matchmaker tale was extended in the fall of 1982 when Tom Stoppard's *On the Razzle* had its American premiere, a comedy drawn upon the 1842 Austrian tale.  John Oxenford's play *A Day Well Spent* opened in London in 1835, followed seven years later in Vienna as a light play by Johann Nestroy, a German adaptation *Einen Jux Will es Machen*.  In 1938 Thornton Wilder adapted the story for the unsuccessful

Broadway play *The Merchant of Yonkers*, starring Jane Cowl. In 1954 he totally revised the play now called *The Matchmaker*, successfully portrayed by Ruth Gordon in London, followed by a long Broadway engagement, but a 1958 Paramount film version starring Shirley Booth failed commercially. The most famous rendition was as *Hello, Dolly!*, the mid-sixties musical version starring Carol Channing.

After Channing, the star vehicle's heroines were Mary Martin, Ginger Rogers, Martha Raye, Eve Arden, Betty Grable, Dorothy Lamour, Yvonne deCarlo, Pearl Bailey, Phyllis Diller and Ethel Merman. The actual musical role of the meddling widow who blithely interfered in the lives of those she sought to influence had been written for Broadway's grande dame Ethel Merman. She did not portray the musical matchmaker until 1970, the end of a long line of Dollys and the performer's farewell to Broadway.

Dolly Levi was originally envisioned as a mature widow who casts the perfect marriages between eligible spouses. When she is commissioned to find a wife for the small town's most successful businessman, the "half-a-millionaire" Horace Vandergelder, it is instead the match Dolly Levi seeks to make for herself. The plot is further complicated by Dolly's romantically manipulating Vandergelder's family and employees.

*Hello, Dolly!* was predicted as being the last of a vanishing species of the Big Event super-costly film musicals. For the most part, these forecasts have proven true, other than, for example, *The Wiz* and *Annie*, which were, significantly, two heavyweight musicals with lightweight box office. The studio's original $12-15 million dollar budget was swollen to $25,000,-000 by the time of Lehman's first script, the financing doubled by overproduction and interest costs. Then the budget was inflated by intense pre-production, including audition interviews with 1,500 actors, singers and dancers. Despite its colossal superstructure, the original plans were even more lavish, each element being trimmed to an anticipated $20 million expenditure.

The potent potential of the famed musical filmed with a burgeoning budget guaranteed that only a colossal performer would be immortalized as Dolly Levi, and the Streisand casting was rumored for weeks, finally confirmed by studio chieftain Richard Zanuck in May 1967. *On a Clear Day You Can See Forever* was considered an inevitable film musical for the superstar musical actress, but the *Dolly!* coup was quite a surprise. Even the producer Ernest Lehman noted that they debated six months before asking agent David Begelman to discuss *Dolly!* with his client. Streisand is perfectly matched to the matchmaking role in performing ability and with the heroine's aggressive personality. But initially she did not take the studio's suggestion seriously, knowing that, as written, the Broadway musical farce would be wrong for her. The moguls countered her objections by promising to make the show more substantial and to add more songs, and for a young star the film focus was altered to feature the matchmaker's own romance, reaching back to the original sources for more weight.

Still uninterested in the role, Streisand told her agent to request a vast sum of money, finally relenting when the Fox moguls agreed. The studio's one-picture contract was the largest ever given to a beginning actor (*Funny Girl* cameras not having rolled yet), the upfront salary of $750,000 not including profits, deferred points from the box office and soundtrack keeping her price artificially low. When Streisand would later seek legal means for not fulfilling her contract, she had to accept the fact that the studio would have sued her and most likely gotten an injunction.

Instead of filming *Wait Till the Sun Shines, Nellie* and a musical version of *Two for the Seasaw* for Ray Stark, the actress was also said to have tried to cancel her binding Rastar contract by filming for 20th Century-Fox first, causing a legal confrontation. Stark feared she would never be available for him and his own injunction was filed in January 1968. Rastar contended breach of contract for Streisand's CBS-TV work during the *Funny Girl* production, seeking an accounting of her proceeds from the Central Park and Hollywood Bowl concerts. She proceeded with the rival studios' films but finally accepted *The Owl and and the Pussycat*, after which Stark dropped the litigation.

Cynics have wondered if perhaps, even subconsciously, Streisand finally consented to play *Dolly!* because of Carol Channing's having won the Tony Award for the original Broadway version, ousting Streisand's *Funny Girl* performance. But actually the younger star had believed initially that only Channing should immortalize the role, and she was very pleased to receive a gracious congratulatory note and flowers. Then on the road with the same musical, Channing sent a bouquet of yellow roses and a telegram, "So happy for you and Dolly, dearest Barbra. Love, Carol." Her tactful note was naturally publicized, and the recipient noted, "I called my husband right away and told him about it, very excited. He said, `Yes, I already read about it in the paper.'" [7-2-67 *L.A. Times* When Channing realized that she would not be cast, she diplomatically announced, "I'm glad that, if I didn't get it, so young and decided a talent as Miss Streisand would."

The studio received more than a few protest letters over the Broadway originator's being overlooked as Dolly. Channing's singularity might be attributed to the fact that she did not seem to be acting the role but seemed that she was Dolly Levi. The studio had apparently not accounted for the stage actress' having a substantial following, heightened after having taken the musical on the road, and some people resented what was perceived, erroneously, as a superstar actress' takeover. Channing's offbeat personality and gravely voice served her well on the stage but were never captured by the overly-familiar Hollywood cameras, which made her seem overbearing and even misbegotten to the film-makers.

Lehman told a reporter that the studio made the best choice and that he would not become the scapegoat for whatever backlash occurred. "I'm rather amused, in fact, by the manipulated anti-Streisand campaign represented in letters received here at 20th, because of their startling similarity in wording. It's just too much of a coincidence, even though they come from various parts of the country." The producer defended the youthful Streisand as Dolly Levi because Thornton Wilder had specified an "uncertain age" for his heroine. [5-22-67 *L.A. Times*]

The press protested that Streisand was too shy and introverted to portray the irrepressible, outgoing matchmaker who was meant to be an Irishwoman at that. The casting was attacked as Hollywood's typically commercial signing of the biggest star possible and not necessarily the appropriate choice. The late Gower Champion was similarly excluded when Michael Kidd was selected as choreographer.

However much Carol Channing was excellent on Broadway, she could never have exceeded any Streisand performance. The category was musical performer, and the singing actresses cannot even be compared. The injustice done was in dishonoring a controversial personality, the Barbra Streisand scandal, of sorts, erupting during the *Funny Girl* filming. Ironically, considering the row over the youthful casting, *Dolly!* had been a stage role which aging stars had used to resurrect their careers.

Several weeks after signing, the actress became quite panicky about being the wrong age for the middle-aged matron, calling Lehman in the middle of several sleepless nights to ask what she was doing in such a film. She thought the character's anguish was that of a woman losing her youth and thus urgently seeking her own marital match, but her own youth was to force upon her a younger characterization not in keeping with the story. Streisand always knew she was the wrong age: "I did feel that *Dolly!* was a story of older people and that they should hire Elizabeth Taylor to play her." It was her opinion that as the mature dramatic actress' vehicle, *Dolly!* would be ideal for her first musical.

Although Streisand did not identify with the matchmaking meddler that is Dolly Levi, she did understand the character's enthusiasm for managing a budget, and despite her young years, the actress knew too that she had loved and lost, private thoughts she never explained. "But I really didn't respond to the Broadway show-- a piece of fluff." The opposition she encountered about the casting finally challenged her to accept, but the kind of role which really appealed to her was Medea. "Dolly takes place in an age before people realized they hated their mothers-- the whole Freudian thing." She knew she could not discover any deep psychological insight but that she could have a good time playing Dolly Levi.

As a Hollywood star, Streisand recognized that she was finally powerful enough to impose her artistic instincts on the film-makers, and yet she disliked such behavior, preferring to work with the creative forces who either agreed or could convince her otherwise, which she discovered was a great time-saver. The actress appreciated the Fox film-makers for valuing her contributions more than Stark had. In one of their long telephone discussions about the script, Streisand asked Lehman if she could pronounce her late husband's name Ephraim with a long and not short initial vowel. He also altered the word "particularly" to "especially" when he agreed with her that the former word was a tongue-twister in one distinctly fast-talking scene.

For the first time the famous Thornton Wilder story was not a romantic fantasy but a realistic romance. Opened out for the widescreen, the comedy was not as broad, although the photography was meant to be as bright and airy as possible.

The film-makers meant for *Dolly!* to stick to Hollywood traditions, the standard movie musical fare in which the orchestra is magically invisible when the stars sing and dance outdoors, the townspeople participating as in instant chorus.

Streisand had chosen Kelly as director, but a muted rivalry was involved in having given a noted choreographer, Michael Kidd, responsibility for the dance direction when the film director was himself a famous dancer. Kelly later admitted being concerned about the rumor that Streisand had had people fired from film productions but could find absolutely no evidence to support the charge. Not having directed a musical since *Invitation to the Dance* in 1956, Kelly travelled to New York to discuss the picture with the star, delighted by her store of ideas. He easily resolved the rumors he kept hearing by this one meeting when he bluntly asked, "Barbra, is there any truth to all these stories that you don't want to rehearse and that you're difficult?" Her dignified response: "No." Declaring how eager she was to play Dolly, she requested only that a director give her guidance.

Kelly bragged about the star, "She's a worker and an indefatigable trouper. I found her attack exciting. Many actors concentrate solely on their performances. Barbra does this, but she also wants to know what the effect will be." [4-69 *Action!*] Many years later Streisand confided how distressed she had been when the director had had no reply to her inquiry about his cinematic concept of the musical. Because of all the possible options she envisioned, she was baffled. "I thought it could have been a wild film," she apologized. [11-13-83 *Herald Examiner*]

*Dolly!* executive Gene Taft noted of the perfectionist: "She sees color breakup on the nash; she can see the color within colors. She can carry on five different conversations at one time with five different people and not lose her place." [12-77 *ViewPoint*] Musical director Lionel Newman was impressed with the star's professionalism when she insisted on studying three of the score's songs on a day when her voice was affected by a serious cold.

Composer-lyricist Jerry Herman's score was amplified for the soundtrack. To make Dolly a warmer and more lifelike woman and to utilize the singer's higher vocal range, the film-makers added the ballad "Love is Only Love," eliminating "Motherhood." Both Zanuck and Lehman were appalled that Jerry Herman, instead of writing a new song as he had agreed, recycled a *Mame* outtake and still charged a fortune.

The musical's excellent songs overall were overshadowed by the catchy staging of the title song, although Streisand had dismissed the Broadway original, especially disdainful of the audience panting "for that one song," a simple number which seemed the least appealing to her. She intended to embellish on film what she considered an underrated but excellent score as a whole, although her preferred songs-- "Ribbons Down My Back" and "It Only Takes a Minute"-- belonged to other singers.

In one of its articles, *Time* commented: "[Jerry Herman's] score for *Hello, Dolly!* seems to contain the strains of nothing but borrowed memories. Indeed, even his title song was publicly conceded to be derived from another tune by another man." [12-26-69] Herman paid an estimated one-quarter to one-half million dollars in settlement to composer Mack David for admittedly using the melody from his popular 1940's song "Sunflower." The "Hello, Dolly!" writer retained the rights to his song, the judgment being that he apparently borrowed the melody accidentally. Equally questionable is the fact that an early-century British song had also been called "Hullo, Dolly Gray!"

With *Funny Girl* due to begin filming July 5, 1967, *Hello, Dolly!* was planned with an early 1968 start-date, and the actress went rather quickly from one picture to another, returning to Hollywood mid-February for the subsequent musical's fittings and rehearsals, the filming having been moved to mid-April. The 90-day schedule was completed August 23, the production involving Streisand for six months. On April 24 Elliott Gould had given his 26-year-old wife a surprise birthday party, in her trailer, and that same day she herself surprised the cast and crew with token gifts. On Mother's Day Gould coached Jason in memorizing a chorus of "Hello, Dolly!", which he warbled to his mother that morning, prompted by Dad. Streisand said only a mother would have recognized the melody.

A modest bungalow served as the star's dressing room on the set, and she was amused that the studio personnel seemed surprised by her not requesting a special arrangement, wondering if they feared a temperamental actress making infinite demands. She would later recall, "It was very difficult doing *Dolly* because they never saw me. They [had] only heard about me. There were all these ridiculous stories and people tend to believe them, as I believe the things I read. It's the power of the printed word." [1-12-69 *London Sunday Times*]

The actress had been persuaded to socialize more, appearing at the home of Paul Newman and Joanne Woodward for a Senator Eugene McCarthy fund-raising cocktail party and being photographed departing with the candidate. On the tenth of April, she presented the best song Oscar at the Academy Awards, her first such participation in the crucial rite of Hollywood. The actress' appearance caused a rash of talk, that she really was unphotogenic after all, her curly wig not at all well received. The young actress sensed that people in Hollywood hated her for being so successful, even though they pretended to be so loving and helpful.

On May 20, Joyce Haber's "girl monster" piece appeared in the newly-launched NEW YORK magazine. The woman alleged that Streisand was not only a tyrant but also boring, as well as bored, if she were not the constant focus of attention, far from the truth for any rather shy person. Columnist Liz Smith also wrote a lengthy article based upon a series of interviews at the time which the *New York Times* cancelled when Streisand exercised her previously agreed-upon right of quote approval. The star believed that the editors rejected a favorable depiction, as a "puff piece."

Streisand "by-lined" an article in *Celebrity* newspaper about her cupid role, "My Search for Dolly Levi," most likely an interview excerpted as a monologue. For the first time she was approaching a role she had not done before, although it was a personal interpretation she had contemplated at length. In the "spontaneous medium" of film, she allowed as much of herself to emerge as her instinct judged correct. She had had one obstacle to overcome initially: "I didn't want to play this role because the part of `Dolly' that is me, is a part of me I don't like to be shown.

"You see, it is the story of any woman who has loved and lost and has to make that important decision whether to live the rest of her life or just dwell on the past and memories. And that's a very universal problem to women of all ages. This woman is a widow, but this doesn't mean she has to be old. After all, she could be a widow of 19, married a year, who'd lost her husband in a war." She appreciated a reporter's description of herself as half-aristocratic and half-street urchin-- and knew that her dream roles would be, for example, the colorful and sinful courtesans of the 1800's, or noted authors in history. Dolly Levi seemed rather unglamorous, but she accepted the outgoing characterization finally for what she was, enjoying the task of choosing the kind of basic jewelry Dolly would wear.

After the first day's rushes she felt more secure in the role, altering her interpretation somewhat so that the woman came to be a more accurate portrayal. "I first felt I was making a mistake with her. I wasn't really relating to myself. It was too much of a `white bread' performance-- meaning I was trying not to be too `New York.' I was a little too elegant for Dolly." She understood that she did not have to disguise the

Barbra Streisand element of her characterization-- she knew then that she would succeed.

It was the starring actress who would bear the sole responsibility for the multi-million dollar studio investment, and she explained her natural anxieties to a reporter, asking rhetorically, "If this were your second film, and there was a fortune backing it, how would you feel? Everyone expects me to behave like a star, but deep down I hate having to smile when I don't want to, to hide what I really feel." [1-70 *Photoplay Film Monthly*] She did appreciate the relaxed shooting schedule: "You know, I have so much time off this time. Dolly doesn't really do much in this picture." [Earl Wilson column]

After wearing 41 costumes in *Funny Girl* and being needed for every scene, she only wore six outfits in her second musical and was even allowed days off.

Instead of being present in scene after scene-- which one might assume about this famous role-- the title character is often absent while the unusually predominant supporting characters develop their own stories.

Streisand effected a long, deliberate stride for her characterization and also evoked another of her favorite role models, Rita Hayworth in *Strawberry Blonde*. The actress was regarded as being so skeptical of her role that she was distanced from Dolly Levi, seemingly very irreverent. Her interpretation would be said to be flawed: comic acting implausibly offset with the too realistic and sober singing which she had prerecorded before finalizing the heroine in her mind. Being so insecure about the basic casting, it was only natural that the actress reached for various colors of characterization, and it would eventually be alleged that she camouflaged the age differential by camping the role to excess.

Streisand learned to glance at the director after each take to see whether he flashed a thumbs up or down sign. Ernest

Lehman told Kelly's biographer Clive Hirschhorn that Streisand lost confidence in the director when he could not help her with her interpretation of her role, causing tension in their relationship and communication. Kelly felt that she did not recognize his status as a musical and dance veteran, which Lehman said she acknowledged but not openly.

The director told his biographer, "If only there had been more time, I'd have tried to help her work out a clear-cut characterization. But we had a tight schedule and I left it up to her. The result was she was being Mae West one minute, Fanny Brice the other, and Barbra Streisand the next. Her accent varied as much as her mannerisms. She kept experimenting with new things out of sheer desperation, none of which really worked to her satisfaction. And as she's such a perfectionist, she became neurotic and insecure." His insufficient time excuse is weak; with the monumental effort applied, some concern should have been the all-essential question of the acting.

The director and star did work overtime on the characterization a couple of early weekends, Streisand telling reporters that her most exciting *Dolly!* experiences had been dancing on the set (off-camera) with the famous song-and-dance man. He realized that despite her insecurity and anxiety, she zealously maintained a positive attitude, as did he; Kelly was determined to maintain his cheerful, optimistic façade, the opposite of the producer's characteristic gloom and doom demeanor. The director believed that Zanuck was disinterested in budget restraints when *The Sound of Music* had been so immensely profitable.

Marianne McAndrew played the part of Irene Molloy, Vandergelder's would-be arrangement, and in the grand tradition of Hollywood, her singing was dubbed. Ambrose Kemper, the frustrated suitor of Vandergelder's niece, was played by Tommy Tune, the 6'6" actor and later the famous director and star of Broadway musicals such as *Nine* and *My*

*One and Only*.   Co-star Michael Crawford, who played Vandergelder's employee, Cornelius, praised his colleague to the press, having dismissed all the warnings of difficulty, as he found Streisand's extreme timid nature and loneliness to be caused by the distant reverence from other people.  She confided to him her pleasure in being invited to a party by the chorus girls in the London stage version of *Funny Girl*, Crawford grasping the irony that her image made her seem too important to mingle with others, and then she believed they were avoiding her.

The actor remembered his clowning during filming, often swearing in jest.  "Barbra would pretend to be shocked: `Just listen to him,' she'd call out.  `That sweet voice and the dreadful things he says!'"  His attitude changed after the London premiere of her first movie *Funny Girl* (during which the two *Dolly* comrades had been unable to speak to each other).  Crawford began complaining that she was unprofessionally tardy on the set, keeping the cast and crew waiting, whereas co-star Walter Matthau had been always punctual. Two decades later Michael Crawford starred in the famous London and Broadway musical, *The Phantom of the Opera*.

In 1969, when Streisand was feted by the Friars Club, *Hello, Dolly!* producer Ernest Lehman wrote a souvenir program tribute facetiously entitled *Who Needs Her?*  He complained that the woman was always harping about some observation or another and "too often she's RIGHT, dammit. And she makes the point by poking you in the ribs with that long, tapering index finger of hers and it hurts."  The "roast" proceeded as Lehman protested her habit of eating from his plate, especially when he was hungry.  "What kind of behavior is this?  And then one day she DOESN'T eat off your plate and you get depressed.  It's ridiculous."  With his dual role of producer-writer, Lehman said he was particularly vulnerable to her long late-night calls to discuss the picture.  "But to talk to him for an HOUR?...  TWO hours?... just to make a few scenes BETTER?... just to make the WHOLE PICTURE better?"

# Chapter 16

"Walter Matthau's Famous Feud
with Barbra Streisand"

**Hard** words spoken by an actor to an actress, Walter Matthau as Horace Vandergelder to Barbra Streisand's Dolly Levi: "Wonderful woman." A loveable grouch, Matthau is a normally likeable character actor who has appeared in over fifty films. But the *Hello, Dolly!*'s co-stars had several clashing encounters during the production, a well-publicized but one-sided feud from a man whose wailing and griping seem to be a chronic condition. The often fiery fighting between the co-stars has become legend, and in later years the actor accepted responsibility for the skirmishes.

A still-bitter Walter Matthau remembered the tempest a couple years after filming during an interview with the *Chicago Tribune*'s Gene Siskel:

> I took the part to build up my salary. There was a strange kind of attraction to the fact that I was going to work with Streisand. I almost knew that I was going to blow up at her.
> I tried very hard, very hard to be civil, but it's extraordinarily difficult to be civil to her. See, she's a soloist, and she likes to tell the conductor when the flutes come in, when the violins come in.
> When she acts-- and I say that in quotes-- she likes to tell the director when the other actors should

come in. She pretends as though she's asking, but she's overstepping her boundaries. She should simply be the instrument of the director, and not be conductor, the composer, the scene designer, the costume designer, the acting coach, et cetera.

Unfortunately that's what happens when people become stars before they learn their craft.

An actor able to offset Barbra Streisand, Walter Matthau was considered similarly larger-than-life, but an insecure, traumatized and overwrought actress was directly contradictory to the other's cool professional calm. Initially Streisand was delighted to be filming with the Hollywood veteran who said that he accepted the role when curious about the new experience of a musical and about working with so celebrated a singer. She was quickly frustrated by her co-star's unfounded public paranoia that she was "prejudiced against him from the beginning."

It was the actor's attitude which had been distorted even before the beginning, having unfortunately been told poisonous tales by the Broadway *Funny Girl* lead actor Sydney Chaplin who related his own misadventures. Streisand especially resented Matthau's hostile humor, ridiculing her nose when they had accidentally met a few years prior. In 1965 Streisand made a backstage visit to Piper Laurie in a Millburn, New Jersey revival of *The Glass Menagerie*. When Matthau also stuck his head in the dressing room, he glanced at Streisand and said, "Oh, you must be Barbara Harris. You ought to get that nose fixed," as she remembered the acerbic introduction. [11-13-83 *L.A. Herald Examiner*] "I was so shocked, I couldn't even answer him."

Matthau's version is that he had decided to be devilish to avenge the stories he had heard by asking, "Oh, you're Barbara Harris. I see you've had your nose done."

At the time of filming he told a reporter, "We don't talk much outside the scenes. I say: `To hell with you,' and she says, "To hell with you!' We're perfectly matched." [1-70 *Photoplay Film Monthly*]

During their battles that summer he called her "Madame Ptomaine," possibly referring to the old-word usage for food poisoning, and she called him "Old Sewer-Mouth," at one point parrying with a bar of soap, "That's to wash your mouth out." Astonished by his behavior, the actress wondered what could possibly be wrong with the man. She also confided that she missed working with her *Funny girl* co-star Omar Sharif: "He is very conscientious and always a gentleman. He is never petty or like a vain actor. And he's always a man." [Summer 1968 *Women's Wear Daily*] We can read any meaning we choose into such a statement.

Walter Matthau evidently feared playing a stubborn, crotchety bachelor alongside a sexy young widow, making him feel old and boring. The man's exasperating personality was apparent early in the production, such as an encounter with her son during a rendition of the title song. When Jason was brought to his mother on the restaurant set, the actor gruffly joked to the infant, "Only way to bring up kids is to talk baby talk to 'em and beat 'em." The mother seemed uncomfortable and said that her son would ride in the car, and her co-star retorted, "Gonna make poopoo in the car, Jason?" [5-6-68 Earl Wilson column]

Early in the production Matthau uncouthly told a visiting reporter, "She steps on your head and your tail. She's gotta wave her goddarn feathers across your balls and in your eyes, otherwise she's not happy." Matthau objected not only to the star's tardiness but to the time she required to get into character. He constantly complained of being made to wait while the star was meticulously prepared and lighted for the shooting, although it was not her responsibility that several hours were required to fix her elaborate hairstyles, makeup and costumes.

Streisand asked Matthau one day, "How's your ulcer?"

"I don't have an ulcer," he replied.

"My maid said she heard on the radio that I was giving you an ulcer."

"You may be giving me another heart attack, darling, but not an ulcer." [*Esquire*]

When Streisand helpfully mentioned a Matthau acting technique which she also felt would better her own performance, he complained, "Cool it, baby. You may be the singer in this picture, but I'm the actor." After listening to another of the actress' suggestions, he shouted angrily, "Why don't you let the director direct?"-- and she returned, "Why don't you learn your lines?" He acidly retaliated, "You don't have to be great all the time, do you?"

With the director and producer supporting the indispensable actress, the actor complained to 20th Century's Richard Zanuck, who was unable to pacify him. The actor is popularly said to have complained that he would surely suffer from a heart attack because of Streisand. "I'd like to help you out, but the film is not called *Hello, Walter!*," the studio mogul replied.

In a provocatively quotable account, Walter Matthau later told *Gene Kelly* biographer Clive Hirschhorn that Streisand did not attempt to compromise with him, and so he would not do the same with her.

> The trouble with Barbra is she became a star long before she became an actress. Which is a pity, because if she learned her trade properly she might become a competent actress instead of a freak attraction - like a boa constrictor. The thing about working with her was that you never knew what she was going to do next and were afraid she'd do it. I found it a most unpleasant picture to work on and, as most of my scenes were with her, extremely distasteful. I developed all kinds of symptoms. Pains in the lower abdomen, severe headaches, palpita-

tions: I was in agony most of the time. I wish I could figure out exactly what happened to me, but I haven't been able to yet. All I remember and know is that I was appalled by every move she made. I was in a terrible fright and in a state of shock most of the time. Once I heard her tell Lennie Hayton, our musical director, that the flutes were coming in too soon, and that the first violins were too fast. Then she started telling Gene how she thought I should feed her lines. Gene, meantime, was trying to placate her and, like a good director, to keep the peace. He should, of course, have told her to mind her own business and do as she was told and not pay so much attention to other people as she had a lot to learn herself. And when she had twenty years more experience, then she should still shut up because she wasn't the director. The poor girl was corrupted by power in her second movie!

Unfortunately, I'm rather slow to fight back. I'll adjust, assimilate and give ninety per cent in order to make something work. I will totally submerge myself or turn my back if someone needs the stage or the camera. And I hasten to add that I don't do this because I'm such a wonderful, self-sacrificing guy. It's sheer vanity on my part. I think I'm such a good actor, you see, it doesn't matter what the hell I do! At the same time I'm helping the other person in the picture or the play or whatever. But when the other person abuses this and takes it all as a sign of weakness, that's when I fight back and lose my temper. And the realization, as *Hello, Dolly!* progressed, that I'd agreed to take a supporting role to a beginner probably didn't help matters either."

Their big squabble occurred when Streisand insisted that a wrapped scene could be improved, even though Matthau and the director were satisfied, the row erupting when Kelly finally yielded to his star about reshooting. "Everybody in this company hates you! All right, walk off! Just remember, Betty Hutton once thought she was indispensable," Matthau taunted her. Although the monster legend claims that the crew applauded the actor's words, a review of the record reveals how clearly wrong he was, how boldly self-incriminating his remarks are.

The Cold War had erupted into overt hostilities when the tension was severely worsened by the tragic death of Democratic presidential candidate Robert F. Kennedy. Those early June 1968 days the company was on location during sweltering 100° summer weather, production further plagued by filming delays and swarms of mosquitoes. A palatable pall descended over the company with the announcement of the assassination. Matthau colorfully recalled his tirade against Barbra Streisand during the climactic confrontation:

> As if contending with the elements were not enough, Barbra kept asking Gene whether he didn't think it would be better if I did this on this line, and that on the other, etc., etc. - and I told her to stop directing the fucking picture, which she took exception to, and there was a blow-up in which I also told her she was a pip-squeak who didn't have the talent of a butterfly's fart. To which she replied that I was jealous because I wasn't as good as she was. I'm not the most diplomatic man in the world, and we began a slanging match like a couple of kids from the ghetto. I think Gene thought one of us was going to die of apoplexy or something, or that I'd belt her, or that maybe she'd scratch my eyes out - or worse, that we'd just walk off leaving twenty million dollars' worth of movie to go down the toilet.

Matthau interpreted the rout quite differently for writer C. Robert Jennings:

I took it hard. I wasn't going to vote for Bobby Kennedy. Still, I was knocked out and Gene was too. I couldn't work that day - and it was a 100 degrees in Garrison. Giant brutes [high-wattage lights] surrounded us in a complicated outdoor scene. With the Kennedy thing and the heat and all this electrical power my head felt it was being smashed, plus the talk about where the bullet hit, the brain operation and all. Suddenly, Barbra sneezed and I took that as a personal insult. I went into a wild, furious incoherent tirade about her. Kelly put his hand on my arm and tried to pull me away - that's all I remember except that I had to get my lines out, and I did not use any profane language....

Streisand had been shocked and grief-stricken, even angry, as most Americans were about Senator Kennedy's murder, and unlike Matthau, she was going to vote for the brother of her beloved John F. Kennedy. Under the circumstances she must have loathed the entire concept of a film frolic based on *Hello, Dolly!*, Matthau apparently sharing the mood but the tragedy serving only to make him edgier and no closer to the star.

With three hours of filming lost, an uneasy détente was finally established by evening, Streisand and Matthau promising to be at least courteous to each other. She was grievously hurt, and perplexed, wondering why she had to endure his belligerence and bizarre humor. Matthau later remembered that though he was determined to have harmonious relations with the picture's star, the pressure to behave so unnatural to his inclination became almost too intense to bear. He realized that nothing would alter the basic fact that their chemistry was completely wrong. The next day they were urged to say hello to each other, but he rather childishly whined that she should give the first greeting, as he was the older person.

The actor may have said it physically sickened him to work with Streisand, but all she would say to *Playboy*'s Lawrence Grobel was: "I don't like talking about him. It was a long time ago." The interviewer asked if the veteran had been threatened by her. "Perhaps. It was like he was this pro and I was this kid who didn't have any right to any opinions." She admitted her untested four-picture deal had no doubt enraged Matthau and others.

A revelation about the pseudo-feud was confided by the actress during the *Yentl* promotion to her friend, Joseph Morganstern, unlike the *Playboy* interviewer who had probed her unsuccessfully.

> One day I had an idea about something I thought would be funny involving a scene in a wagon. I said, `What do you think of this?' and people started to laugh. But all of a sudden Walter Matthau closed his eyes and started screaming: `Who does she think she is? I've been in 30 movies and this is only her second, the first one hasn't even come out yet, and she thinks she's directing? Who the hell does she think she is?' I couldn't believe it. I had no defense. I stood there and I was so humiliated I started to cry, and then I ran away. And what came out in the papers was Walter Matthau complaining about Barbra Streisand.

Gene Kelly felt that if Streisand had ever offended her co-star, it was unintentionally, even unconsciously, the director dismissing the pivotal fight to columnist Earl Wilson: "It was the classic dispute between actors of who stepped on whose lines. They quarrelled in front of everybody. We went into a little store and straightened it out. Then we did the scene. This happens to everybody in every picture and isn't serious."

He totally denied the stories that Streisand had attacked the actor. "Absurd. I wish every actor would be like her. I came into this picture with my dukes up because I'd heard she could be uncooperative. But she's the most cooperative girl I ever worked with. She'll try anything to be good. There has never been any friction between us and I predict there never will be." [6-24-68] To another reporter Kelly clarified, "No, there's no feud or anything. Walter and Barbra had a fifteen-minute blow-up over who was stepping on whose lines, but since that, Matthau's been putting everybody on about it. He loves people talking about it but he and Barbra are good friends." Desperate comments from the beleaguered director.... Back in Hollywood Matthau's closest concession to an apology was his comment to a reporter: "She is... doing very well for someone so tender in years. She's very young and probably has different values that conflict with other people's. It's very difficult for anyone, let alone a young person, to become a star. They don't leave you alone, you are beset from every angle, and Barbra is not that confident."

The producer Ernest Lehman tactfully described the woman as overly defensive, also telling a reporter, "They quarreled and that lasted a few days. Now, they've kissed and made up. Walter's mother was on the set one day and asked Barbra, `Why do you fight with my son?' and Barbra answered, `He told me he fought with you a lot. I guess he only fights with the people he loves.'" The rapid retort was truly inspired.

Certain he would fail at his first attempts to dance onscreen, the actor was nervous and uncomfortable. "I had a little joke going with Barbra. I tickled her palms in the classic `Do-you-want-to?' tradition and she tickled mine and I was able to do it." The actor resented his co-star's laughing at his recording the title song, but her own defense was quoted in an *Esquire* article about Matthau: "Actually I like the way he sings very much. I don't like male singers, but I like when men sing. It was very charming. I was laughing at Vandergelder the character. I wasn't laughing at Walter." At one time or another he would also concede that she never offered vocal coaching:

"Perhaps she thought I was beyond redemption. She just never spoke up; she's very kind that way."

Streisand wore a Little Orphan Annie wig to the 1968 Academy Awards presentation when she presented the Oscar for best song, but Matthau belittled her, "That hairdo you wore--was that supposed to make the audience laugh?"

"Why are you so cruel? That hairdo is the latest fashion."

"I just wondered if you meant it to be funny."

"You are a very hostile person."

"I don't think I am." [*Esquire*]

At the end of filming Streisand nevertheless gifted her caustic co-star with a memento, having many months earlier found an antique inkwell with a jockey's cap for a top. Knowing the actor's racetrack hobby, she had the horseshoe base inscribed with the greeting, "Walter, I wish you wealth, health, and a little bit of luck, Barbra." A card was signed, "May your horses always come in first." She surprised him with the present when the actor had finished his last scene, Matthau grateful for the gesture but curious, "Why are you giving me a gift?" She replied, "I always give gifts to the people I work with. It's something I thought you might like." Unable to accept any affection from the alienated actress, Matthau later asked a *Dolly!* colleague, "Why didn't she say `I'm giving you a gift because I love you?'"

After the musical was released, the actor said he would rather not say anything about the star if he could not say something good, a kind of refracted tact. He was moved to say at one point, "I had no disagreements with Barbra. I was simply exasperated by her tendency to megalomania." Streisand continued to mourn the anguished relations in later years. "He never did apologize to me and that's what hurt even more. I think the saddest part of what happened was that a man of Walter's stature and ability seemed to feel threatened by me."

The actor does not regret making *Hello, Dolly!* whatsoever, recognizing their basic incompatibility but aware that the trouble was basically the inevitable clashes from artistic differences. He astutely realized that neither they nor their characters were very congenial, excusing the young woman's brashness because of her playing a normally elderly character. His lasting impression was an awareness that his humor can be antagonizing to others if they happen to misunderstand him, and that the press overreacted to several moments of tension. He concluded rather inconclusively, "Barbra had moments of likability. She's a very compelling person."

Looking back in a 1974 interview, the actor analyzed the altercations once more: "She was just too young for the part and she knew it. That's why she made it so difficult for everyone involved. There's nothing more depleting for an actor to feel he's playing the wrong role. You can be gallant about it, but she had too much at stake. I can see it now in perspective. She was a movie star, though none of her films [had] been released. She was insecure, and she couldn't handle it." The actress' own words belie Walter Matthau's interpretation, as she came to believe that she was quite the right age-- and "everyone involved" faulted not her but the bitter and unhappy man.

In later years Matthau grumbled that he did not wish to reopen old wounds, praising his colleague as generous and brilliant and hoping the issue would die. He even admitted the break was his fault but felt that a minor fight had been overblown in its aftermath. He once responded huffily to yet another question about the rumors. "What did you hear? Doesn't it make good copy to have stories like that? Sells tickets, right? *Hello, Dolly!* grossed $48 million, right. Those are stories. What else are we going to talk about?" [Judith Crist's *Take 22 - Moviemakers on Moviemaking*]

To the actor's credit, he apparently realized after Streisand actually directed a film that her talents are deeper than he had suspected. They earnestly talked together for an hour at a Hollywood party after *Yentl*. His wife was one of the most vocal supporters of the film when the original short story writer Isaac Singer ravaged Streisand and her work in the *New York Times*. Walter Matthau was also an invited guest to the singer's Malibu concert in 1986. After fifteen years the actor must have resolved his jealousy, and Barbra Streisand must have gotten her apology. [Sources: Streisand/Matthau quotes include *Esquire*]

# Chapter 17

"Dolly Levi

Immortalized as Barbra Streisand"

More than half of *Hello, Dolly!* was scheduled to be filmed outdoors, the film makers seeking an Upstate New York town suitably old-fashioned in appearance. As the modern-day Yonkers holds few leftovers from its quaint history, the town of Garrison was chosen as its double, located sixty miles up the Hudson River from New York City. The location shooting saved a considerable amount of money which the studio would have spent in recreating the village on a soundstage.

Streisand rented a home for the rural location and between takes read Chaim Potok's novel *The Chosen*. On her own she made some 8-mm footage of the *Dolly!* production. Although she was shy as usual, the actress was quite naturally drawn to the young children in the cast, the fully-costumed star tossing their frisbees back and forth. After the unfortunate Matthau feud climaxed, she tried to isolate herself even more, especially preferring private off-camera moments with her child.

The star was cooled by the breeze from the studio's wind-making fan, and she also carried a small portable fan, vainly trying to escape the heavy moist heat. One day a helicopter down-draft accidentally raised her dress over her head. The actress was bemused by the magic of movies, that none of their intense sweat or dirt would be noticeable onscreen, but she preferred the grittier European near-documentary style. "Our society is based on the make-believe world of films. I think that's why psychoanalysts are so popular here. I remember as a kid, when I came out of a movie I was depressed for days because my life wasn't like the movies." [WWD]

After 27 days on location in June and July, the cast and crew returned to the studio on the 4th of July in three chartered jets, one week behind schedule due to bad weather. Much of the swollen Hollywood budget was consumed on grandiose sets, especially the $2¼ million-dollar Old New York street re-creation, where in mid-July the grand production number "Before the Parade Passes By" was shot in four days at an added cost of $200,000 a day. Half-a-year in construction, the 14-acre outdoor set was the largest and costliest ever construct-ed in film history, despite the parade's mere seven-minute onscreen involvement. The huge Disneylandish set is artificial, lacking a naturally-aged appearance; an angle shot reveals the two-dimensional façade. Like a monument to a relic film, the set was left intact, the popular tourist attraction still standing in a neglected and deteriorating state.

For *Funny Girl* Streisand had sung the climactic song "Don't Rain on My Parade," and this musical's big outdoor production number was called "Before the Parade Passes By." The actress laughed that she was again singing about parades, which she actually disliked. Kelly required endless retakes of the challenging filming, and when a camera boom was jostled by a cable, the actress protested the call for yet another retake. The director explained the problem, but the star grumbled to herself, "The cable is just as important as I am." She also observed ruefully at one point during filming, "Doing this is just like having a baby, very uncomfortable at the time-- but you reckon you'll be proud of your efforts later."

In *Hello, Dolly!*'s pivotal scene, 675 actors and musicians as well as thousands of extras either stood as spectators or marched down the street, the masses coursing across Pico Boulevard into the studio lot in 98° weather. Lehman had visualized a story about the problems between people who link together, and he wanted to create the impression of an individual lost in the crowd. Streisand argued with the director who wanted a final close-up of her singing, the actress insisting that a zoomed-back long-shot should show a barely-visible Dolly being grandly passed by the parade. Kelly finally relinquished, and it is the zoom shot seen onscreen.

The actress also thought she was not getting enough close-ups and told the director so, and she was quite concerned that the cinematography feature her left-hand profile, which she has always believed flatters the bump in her nose. The fifty-year Hollywood cinematography veteran Harry Stradling, now deceased, noted that despite her youth she was hard to film-- but that virtually all her instincts concerning what is right for her were sound. The camera used a sliding soft-focus diffusion glass, the concern being chiefly for her double chins and teen-age acne scars. She was so adept at making up her face that she created a moveable table with lighting compatible to whatever the film crew was using at a given time.

Barbra Streisand does have one prerequisite of great beauty: high and pronounced cheekbones, which were quite evident in Dolly's chiseled face. Nevertheless, she herself complained, "I had three double chins in *Dolly!*. I kept telling people it was because Dolly should be statuesque, but it was a cop-out, because I couldn't diet." The reason her rather slack jaw hardly seemed noticeable was due to a camera angle technique taught by Elizabeth Taylor's cinematographer. "He told me if you hold the cameras up high and shoot down, you don't see the double chins." [1-70 *Life*]

As Dolly, Streisand eliminated the heavy eye makeup and shaped brows which had highlighted her famous sloe-eyed Nefertiti look. The women of the late 1800's would not have been seen in scandalous makeup, so studio makeup official Dan Striepeke had devised "the porcelain look" for the character, untanned and natural, with the wigs dyed a light reddish-blonde to offset the actress' blue eyes. Striepeke studied the artwork of John Singer Sargent's 1890's socialites, the hairstyling brushed high and back reminiscent of Charles Dana Gibson's famed sketches of "The Gibson Girl."

Dolly often looked like a young girl dressed in her grandmother's clothes, although the elaborate costumes were characteristic of the overdone dress of the period. Veteran costumer and five-time Oscar-winner Irene Sharaff wrote in her book *Hollywood Dress Parade*, "Hollywood was curious about Barbra, but people could do little but blink at her." The loquacious and sometimes incoherent actress had opinions and openly stated them about everything, and was at her worst during *Hello, Dolly!* "Her brazen assurance was still in full force and even more tiresome... one day, I asked her why she constantly talked, since it seemed to take so much out of her. She explained that she had to suffer to be able to perform." The down-to-earth costumer once protested, "Oh, stop complaining so much, Barbra, you have everything," but the actress was genuinely hurt. "Oh, but I don't have anything."

Posed for publicity shots lying down in the expensive title number gown, Streisand jested of her horizontal position, "The way every woman should be."

Only the luxurious title song sequence down the wide red staircase could possibly exceed the grand spectacle of the parade which had closed the first act, and much of the musical takes place in the restaurant's art nouveau set decorated at an expense of nearly one million dollars. Streisand was quite self-conscious about the crucial scene, concerned about her dress and her gestures and consulting the director about whether she should bow or wave or spin around the stairway.

Commentators detected more of Streisand herself than of Dolly Levi when singing "Hello, Dolly!" The actress wore a tight-fitting gold lamé gown, feathers in her hair and long white gloves in immortalizing one of the most famous entrances in theatrical history, a song recorded by literally hundreds of singers performed for the first time with matchless gusto and power. Louis Armstrong, playing himself as the restaurant's bandleader, sang a special refrain to and with Dolly, their scat-singing repartee resulting in the true climax of the musical. It had been Armstrong in the early sixties who had originally made a worldwide, Grammy-winning hit of the song. Although Streisand initially thought it cheap and transparent to take advantage of Satchmo to boost the box office, she later changed her mind for what would become a film highlight.

Streisand accepted the public's undeniable fondness for the title song, although it was her least favorite. She added a new interpretation: "I just looked for a way to do it that was in keeping with the character of Dolly. I always thought it should have been a little slower at the beginning, a little out of tempo, dealing more specifically and personally with each one of the waiters. That's the way I did it. Then, of course, it becomes a big thing when they have to sing back to me."

For all the musical's excesses, filming with the stars was completed a day or two before the schedule expected, in late August. Streisand later admitted that she had been bewildered and hurt when her suggestion to hold an end-of-filming party on the set had been discouraged. Instead, Lehman hosted a true surprise party. As always, Streisand gifted her co-stars and crew when the picture wrapped.

The *Dolly!* sets were closed to most outsiders, except certain reporters like Earl Wilson and John Gregory Dunne, the latter writing a book about 20th Century-Fox. Dunne's book, *The Studio*, intimately details the making of several major musicals in the late 1960's, with the chapter devoted to *Hello, Dolly!* It contains an analysis of the troubled shooting by the eventual *A Star Is Born* screenwriter.

When the Broadway showman David Merrick had sold the *Dolly!* motion picture rights for $2 million and a hefty percentage of the profits, the contract stipulated that the studio not release the film until the Broadway run was completed, or six years hence-- until June 20, 1971-- whichever was sooner. This condition was practically disregarded as fine print, more or less, because no one expected the show to run that long. But David Merrick was determined to have the longest-running Broadway musical of all time, and his all-black version with Pearl Bailey gave life to the already extremely healthy box office receipts.

Merrick declared, "They offered money, they threatened to release the picture anyway. They wouldn't dare-- there would be a big injunction." The Broadway impresario said only his pride was involving in making a record, money not being a concern. [2-14-69 *Life*]

The $20 million-dollar film budget required another five million in expenditure for post-production and promotional costs, as well as the interest on the bank loan. With the musical legally shelved for fifteen months, Merrick, who was a major studio stockholder as well and who clearly relished the controversy, finally received more than a million dollars for allowing the pre-1971 release.

Streisand too had been frustrated by the ongoing delays with her second motion picture. The actress must have believed in the commercial potential of *Dolly!* as much as the others did, at least until she saw the colossal studio mismanagement. She became increasingly insecure about all the money lavished on the Great Musical Hope, knowing that it would be difficult to return its investment and that the career most affected would be her own.

Certainly the tempest over Merrick's delaying tactics seemed to cynics to be a mere publicity fabrication, but the problem was real and grave. The print had been left in the film can for over a year while the studio paid $100,000 monthly interest on the financing. The $1 million arrangement with Merrick actually saved money, as the seven-percent interest on the $20 million financing would have accumulated for another year. Instead of *Hello, Dolly!*'s being available as a summer 1969 family extravaganza or even as a 1968 Christmas offering one year after the *Funny Girl* debut, the film makers were forced to wait until very late in the year 1969.

The release of Barbra Streisand's introductory musical trilogy was done on an unbalanced schedule: first *Funny Girl* fifteen months before the next musical, then *Hello, Dolly!* and *On a Clear Day You Can See Forever* necessarily released only six months apart. David Merrick's newspaper ads for the stage show when the film opened stated, "Accept No Substitutes. The Only Truly Authentic Dolly in New York." Streisand wired Ethel Merman an opening-night telegram: "Don't sing too loud. You'll drown me out down the street."

The long-anticipated world premiere to *Hello, Dolly!*-- Dolly Levi immortalized as Barbra Streisand in the celebrated musical-- was held in New York City on December 16, 1969, a $150-ticket benefit for the Police Athletic League. The guests at the Rivoli Theater had to outmaneuver the many fans waiting in freezing temperatures, the general public was excluded from the invitational event. Pressured by the nervous studio into attending the opening to bolster box office receipts, the woman who had become a film goddess with her Academy Award-winning debut in *Funny Girl* caused chaos among the fans and the inadequate security.

Twenty policemen escorted the actress into the theater, where the panicky star felt her physical safety was imperiled. The riotous outdoor crowd of over one thousand ardent admirers had endured the intense cold for hours, and when the star's limousine was spotted, the zealous fans broke through police fortifications and trapped the woman inside the car for five minutes by jostling the vehicle back and forth, blocking traffic. Police were able to force hundreds of the fans into retreating, but the motor procession was slowed to a crawl. The star felt added pressure that the longer she remained safely in her limo, the later the picture would begin. Protected inside the police wedge, it still required fifteen minutes to advance from the car down the red carpet, the star caught in the mad rush into the theater.

Wearing a Mongolian white leather-and-fur creation of Arnold Scaasi, the goddess-heroine was white-faced as she was led from her car amid the crazed fans, the guard lines collapsing just as she made it indoors, the police officers unable to restrain the screaming crowd any longer. Streisand was terrified when a flash exploded near her eyes and the mob turned into a noisy and cursing brawl as fans attacked photographers in the scrimmage. A news photographer stumbled into manager Marty Erlichman, and they scrambled to their feet punching on each other, the actress' manager suffering a bloody gash to his face from a camera, which was destroyed. The ashen and distraught woman shouted, "Oh, my God, what's happening? Marty! Marty! Are you okay, Marty? What did they do to you, Marty?"

As could be expected, Streisand remained panicked by the pandemonium and became quite bitter about the experience, vowing to columnist Earl Wilson, "I will never go to another premiere. It's inhumane. I was devastated by what happened to Marty." Just before the end of the show, a dozen policemen came to escort the star safely from the theater to the Pierre Hotel for the benefit ball, at which Louis Armstrong-- but not Streisand-- sang the title song. Because of a 6:00 a.m. wakeup schedule the next day, the actress was most likely quite relieved to be forced to leave the dinner dance early.

Erlichman escorted his client to the Friday night Chinese Theater premiere on December 19th, three days after the New York premiere. Having been so unnerved by the unruly fans, the studio feared she would not attend the Los Angeles opening, but she was somehow convinced, and survived the west coast showing with added policemen and decoy limousines. *Variety* columnist Army Archerd noted an ecstatic, if skeptical, fan who called the theater to ask if the *Hello, Dolly!* star was really present for the premiere. Following the screening, Streisand had been relaxing in the manager's office and when the fan called, for a lark the star answered the query personally, the fan not realizing her identity until it was too late.

Carefully disguising her fatigue still lingering from the New York premiere and the jet lag from that morning's cross-country flight, Streisand mingled with the other guests at a tent-party until 2:00 a.m., approaching Governor Reagan's table and talking to the First Lady. Matthau was friendly to his one-time rival, greeting the star with a kiss and inviting her to sit at his table, the animosity graciously forgotten. Cameras recorded the apparent cease-fire to the well-publicized battle and the woman's mock protest: "Stop! Stop! You crazy man ... you are absolutely *Crazy!*", she chortled when he clutched her in his arms and gleefully kissed her all over, on her face, hands, arms, neck, chest. Her comments about her co-star were overheard: "He can steal every scene by just raising his eyebrow or with a shrug of those cynical shoulders."

Studio officials released their Christmas season blockbuster musical as a reserved-seat roadhouse attraction, the long running time typical for such a picture: two hours, twenty-eight minutes, twenty-six seconds. Ticket prices were inflated, an intermission was scheduled and souvenir booklets were sold. The advance New York seating, tickets selling as high as $6.50, had been sold out for three months, and the Streisand picture ranked fourth in box office grosses for the year, behind only *Airport*, *M\*A\*S\*H* and *Patton*. *Hello, Dolly!* returned its cost, including the immense interest on the borrowed negative financing, but the musical would have had to bring in nearly three times its investment to return its actual expenditure to the distributor studio after the theaters deducted their rental charges. To show a paper profit the musical needed to make $75 million, which would have been historical box office success in late 60's dollars.

*Dolly!*'s box office income was heavy for a few weeks, the studio trumpeting in industry trades that the receipts exceeded even *The Sound of Music* figures, but eventually the costly roadside picture was considered too expensive for the families to whom it was directed. *Star!*, *Dr. Doolittle*, *Darling Lili* and *Paint Your Wagon* were all the last of the obsolete roadshow genre, although *Hello, Dolly!* was certainly more successful than any of the other musicals. With Hollywood censorship far less restrictive, audiences had changed, the new youthful market more drawn to *Easy Rider* and *Midnight Cowboy* than such wholesome, old-fashioned family fare as the benign Streisand musical.

The dangerously overextended studio was ailing financially before the musical even opened, after nearly going bankrupt with *Cleopatra* and its other musicals. *Hello, Dolly!* only moderately salvaged the struggling Fox studio. *Dolly!*'s outrageous $20 million risky budget can be more properly assessed when contrasted to the *Funny Lady* and *A Star Is Born* musical productions, both budgeted at only $8 million and $6 million, respectively, and still considered rather excessive in the seventies at that price. With 1969 dollars, $20-24 million would convert into more than twice the amount today. Even *Yentl*, fifteen inflationary years later, only cost $16 million.

A musical designed for family audiences, a pre-sold picture if ever one existed, the *Hello, Dolly!* title was familiar to millions. That the stage version was still successful when the film opened is testament to the confidence the studio executives must have assumed would be their triumph with such a property and with such a hot star, but unfortunately, after six long years the public appetite had apparently lessened. Over fifty women had played the heroine in New York and on the road by the time the film opened-- possibly the oversold, overly familiar material was actually unwelcome to the public despite such a dilly of a Dolly. Even Carol Channing regarded the picture as a breathtaking circus, tactfully describing the rival actress to columnist Joyce Haber, "I thought she did the best job she could do."

The overwhelmingly dated *Hello, Dolly!* was an anachronism of old-fashioned traditions in the new hippie era. Veteran Golden Age film-makers had given the musical an unmistakable imprint which was rather jarring in that harshly realistic period. To his credit, Gene Kelly opposed the grand larger-than-life road show musical the studio envisioned as its financial godsend. The director preferred instead an intimate musical of the lightweight story, but the hired film maker's wishes were subordinate to the powerful moguls.

Kelly had suspected that *Hello, Dolly!* was too long, somewhat, but then audiences had loved the show for years... The musical's 2½-hour running time (a long three hours when later broadcast) featuring many non-Streisand scenes would have easily benefitted from minor surgery. The cat-and-mouse plot is just too thin to support an overlong movie, but perhaps if the footage had been condensed, as would *On a Clear Day*, it might have been more accessible to the general public.

The studio would not have shortened a film starring the actress whose *Funny Girl* debut was being released in wide circulation on Christmas Day, but Paramount Studios decided to cut *On a Clear Day* based on the 20th Century-Fox experience. Ironically, the latter musical with its complex plot would have been improved in its longer state as originally filmed. Had *On a Clear Day* been released first, as scheduled, perhaps *Hello, Dolly!* would not have been so overblown. Gene Kelly never directed another musical, and studio vice-president Richard D. Zanuck was ousted partially for having squandered a fortune on *Hello, Dolly!* overspending.

The 20th Century-Fox soundtrack peaked at #49, although it was charted for a long 33 weeks. The picture netted, domestically, $15.2 million, and its worldwide box office repaid the original investment, eventual grosses being over $20 million and enhanced by broadcast and video sales. Film scholars have generally agreed that it was only Streisand who earned as much money as *Dolly!* actually grossed. Over the years the campy cult favorite was further able to recoup its excessive production costs, proving its longevity in a specific film genre. The film became recognized as a landmark: the last of a dying breed at a turning point, the grand finale of the truly spectacular musical epics. Everyone in Hollywood knew that never again would a musical be created of such unrestrained excess.

Streisand played her Jewish mama Dolly Levi as an occasional Mae West tribute against Walter Matthau's grouchy W.C. Fields demeanor. Some critics accepted these mannerisms in the campy characterization as inevitable, but Mae West bitterly resented the impersonation. She complained when the *Myra Breckenridge* studio gave her the dressing room of their *Hello, Dolly!* star, insisting that she was the bigger star and had to have her own room, and so it was redecorated.

Miss West protested during a *Playboy* interview:

> Streisand has the unmitigated gall to imitate me. It'll hurt my *Diamond Lil*, which I'm bringin' to the screen again, in color and with new music. Streisand conflicts with her. If it wasn't for *Dolly* being at Fox, too, I think I'd have gone in there and had 'em take some of it out. She needs a little sex quality in there and she knows imitatin' me is the best way she can get it. But she'd better forget it.

Asked about Streisand's comment that she had wanted to meet Mae West-- in the very early 60's before she was even a star-- but did not wish to disturb her, Ms. West groused, "She didn't wanna bother to ask if she could imitate me-- take it and ask after. Well, it might interest her to know that David Merrick wanted me to do *Dolly*. But I didn't wanna be a Dolly. I'm me. I'm unique." When pressed, she avoided the issue about having always been impersonated, answering illogically that she appreciated the gay imitators. "At a drag ball here recently, there were 16 Mae Wests and not one of that other woman. I always win the prizes, too." [1-71 *Playboy*]

What is so fascinating about being Mae West is that for many decades she was heralded for being the woman of outrageous star behavior, and she succeeded on those terms, Mae West by definition. It is astounding that she really believed what she was saying.

Surely Streisand would have been told of the older woman's feelings before approaching her later in the year at a party hosted by Paul Newman and Joanne Woodward at their home. Finally meeting the legendary Miss West as two peers on equal ground, the young actress humbly knelt at the aged star's feet and exclaimed, "Oh, it's wonderful to see you! I've adored you always." With an icy edginess, West suggested, "Then stop imitating me." Streisand replied, "Oh, I do it because I've always admired you." West jealously retorted, "Baby, cut out the adoration. I invented the Mae West style and I wanted to keep it exclusively for myself." Where could the dialogue have gone after that devastating introduction which must have grievously wounded the insecure Streisand?

*Hello, Dolly!* took an enviable seven Oscar nominations, the prestigous best picture and six "technical" awards: best adapted score; art direction; cinematographer; film editing; costume design; sound. Studio politics notoriously influenced these results as though competing for presidential delegates, heavily pushing the picture with blatant advertising and cultivating votes from each Academy member with private screenings and lavish food. Telephone campaigning and promotional copies of the soundtrack also helped to receive the token recognition which the public relations office knew would give the picture added financial success. The studio trumpeted its best picture nomination as the only such film with a G-rating and the only nominee made in Hollywood. The picture won four of the seven nominations. The best picture loss was to *Patton*, whose star, George C. Scott, boycotted the entire awards ceremony as "a hypocritical cattle show".

Although Streisand was for the second time the recipient of *Cue* magazine's Ninth annual Entertainer of the Year award, she was overlooked for an Oscar nomination, so soon after having won less than a year prior. Not being nominated must have been a disappointment but one for which the musical's mixed reception had prepared her. Streisand participated in the April 7, 1970 ceremony, presenting to John Wayne his best actor Oscar. Elliott Gould was nominated as best supporting actor for *Bob & Carol & Ted & Alice*, and with the alienated spouse having become an independent star and *Dolly!* not the blockbuster smash expected, gratified gossips were gleeful.

*Hello, Dolly!* looms so colossal on the widescreen that it necessarily lessened the impact of the Streisand performance, the sets and scenery eclipsing the star. The lesson of big screen musicals not learned by the film makers was that being too closely tied to the soundstage denied the musical story its vibrancy, the picture perceived as too stagey. The constant spectacle became tiresome to watch, too much of a good thing. It was said that the actress was too full of life to be convincing as a widow who had gone into seclusion. Streisand herself disliked the musical afterwards.

Despite all the hoopla about imitating Mae West, it was only an infrequent mocking of the sex symbol, Dolly Levi being uniquely Streisand's own multi-layered characterization. Other than the campy and flashy undertones, the actress played a bravura role somewhat more charmingly and pleasantly than originally conceived for the stage. The indefatigable cupid was portrayed with a slight Southern belle accent, an arch Brooklyn accent, campy bits of Sadie Thompson, a little of Lillian Russell, a bit of Lena Horne, and "brassily elegant," as it was said. Columnist Joyce Haber even alleged that the actress mimicked Sue Mengers for part of her manipulations. Too many role models, and she had none.

The picture's notices were clearly divided, the negative voices evenly matched with the positive portrayals. Many critics were astounded with the elaborate package and the dynamic star; others felt overwhelmed. Donald J. Mayerson, *The Villager*: "Miss Streisand is too real and honest a performer to carry off a cartoon character like Mrs. Levi. The part calls for a touch of madness and Miss Streisand is too sane." Some critics considered the actress a counterfeit heroine, cool and detached from the role, which belies her own explanation of the characterization.

The notorious hostility caused by Walter Matthau may have subsequently lessened Streisand's performance. Although it is true that Dolly could have been a young widow, little pathos can be aroused without the onset of a woman's declining years: why would this young woman fear not enticing many men into marriage? Why choose the elderly and irascible Horace Vandergelder? Critics wondered why he finally surrendered to Dolly with no real motivation given. As the sexless romance was described, Horace and Dolly seem to have had a match merely made as a marriage of convenience, but as Dolly's song suggests, "Don't look for shooting stars-- love is only love." Even Gene Kelly would have been a more inspired choice, had he directed himself in the role.

John Simon's first Streisand film review was of *Hello, Dolly!*, harping on the "pronouncedly ugly" star. This was the first of many reviews with an unvarying preoccupation, even obsession, about the actress' looks and personality, with no consideration given to any other aspect of her performances. His pseudo-intellectual writing claimed that the star's following does not merely identify with her but that they transcend her appearance in their self-image. Apparently the critic has been desperately attempting to assuage his own embarrassment at having raved about the unknown woman upon his first sight of the *Wholesale* actress.  His *Dolly!* review:

> A full-face closeup of Miss Streisand is a truly terrifying experience: as the camera moves in tighter and tighter, you know how Edmund Hillary must have felt, and there is no Tenzing Norkay to catch you if you slip, or just reel backward in horror.  As for the star's acting, Machiavelli observed in a letter: `I think that just as nature has given everyone a different face, so she has given to all a different intelligence and imagination, and each acts according to this personality.'  Miss Streisand, perhaps because she lacks intelligence and imagination, is obliged to act according to her face-- aggressively, smugly, and with a masturbatory delight in herself." [Reprinted *Movies Into Film-Film Criticism*, 1967-1970]

# Chapter 18

"`To Me

Being a Real Star is a Movie Star'"

Soon after Barbra Streisand's only child was born in the very
last days of 1966, the actress descended upon Los Angeles in
the spring to make her film debut-- and to alter forever the
course of Hollywood history.  To Streisand the true aura of
stardom was film fame-- the woman had become famous portraying the legendary singer/comedienne Fanny Brice in the
Broadway musical biography *Funny Girl*-- and now in the film
of the same name she would memorialize her smash role on
celluloid.  Fanny Brice is definitely an apt casting for Barbra
Streisand.  The question today-- and almost immediately after
triumphing onstage-- is who could perfectly portray Streisand
in her life story?

Including the semi-biographical *Funny Girl* and *Funny
Lady*, four films have been based upon the life of Fanny Brice.
*Broadway Through a Keyhole* in 1933 with Constance Cumm-
ings and *Rose of Washington Square* in 1939 with Alice Faye
and Tyrone Power.  Both movies featuring period music were
released during Brice's lifetime.  *Funny Girl* was created as a
stylish musical comedy version of Fanny Brice's life, but few
expected Streisand to portray a strictly authentic heroine.

Like Barbara Streisand, Fanny Brice also changed the
spelling of her name, from Fannie to Fanny.  When the young
woman begged composer Irving Berlin for material, he suggested she sing "Sadie Salome" with a Yiddish accent, which

sparked her first success, and then she received a telegram-invitation from the great showman Florenz Ziegfeld. During the 1921 Follies she introduced "My Man," the comedienne having been challenged to make the audiences cry. Holding a shawl to her throat, she sang the emotional torch song against a black velvet drop and a dimly-lighted lamppost.

Fanny's daughter Fran married an agent who became a powerful producer, Ray Stark. Fanny Brice died in 1951 just after completing her memoirs, but Fran was distressed by her mother's too-candid recollections, and her husband bought the book rights for $50,000, having the dictated book plates destroyed. Stark tried unsuccessfully in the fifties to convince Hollywood to make another Brice film, and when he again pitched the biography to the next generation of Hollywood moguls in the early sixties, they were still uninterested. Stark turned to Broadway producer David Merrick, who was intrigued with the project's prospects as a musical, so that Isobel Lennart's *My Man* screenplay was rewritten for the stage as *Funny Girl*.

Possibly *Funny Girl* would have become the longest-running Broadway musical had Streisand stayed in the cast, offering not only a popular show but an assured superstar attraction, but she finally escaped the two-year sentence when her contract expired. To be given the film role, the actress was forced to accept four other pictures for Stark. The producer had always taken it for granted that the great Streisand would film her Brice role, and the actress could have successfully called his bluff, which she surely realized later. "I just felt she was too much a part of Fanny, and Fanny was too much a part of Barbra to have it go to someone else. Sure, there's always an element of risk when you take someone who has never made a film and put her in a $10,000,000 production. But this is *Barbra Streisand*." [2-68 *Cosmo*]

Although the media widely declared that Streisand would receive one million dollars as the largest debut salary ever, in truth Stark carefully restrained his star, knowing he had the upper hand. She was paid only $200,000 and he refused her pleas to grant a percentage of the box office, even in lieu of upfront money. Stark clarified the rumored one million dollar salary as including both the star's income as an actress and her subsidiary rights, such as soundtrack recording royalties.

The 52-year-old producer described their turbulent relationship just before the picture premiered: "It's like the theme of `Funny Girl.' We love each other, but love is not enough." [9-19-68 *N.Y. Times*]

Knowing that without Barbra Streisand no creditable *Funny Girl* could have been created, we can speculate that it was she with the advantage-- but conjecture aside, the facts are that Streisand learned how to be tough from such executive bamboozling. Grobel later questioned the actress about the ambivalent relationship between her and Stark and the long-term indenture which she soon fiercely regretted. Not willing to sacrifice the role of Fanny Brice, she could not insist on just one film at a time, although she was tempted to gamble. She admitted that, in essence, these four projects were to be of Stark's choosing.

The producer envisioned an elaborate, old-fashioned period piece of a musical. Although many studios had abandoned major musicals, others had not, hoping that the once-profitable genre would once again earn big money, epic musicals offered as an antidote to the powerful audience appeal of television, the new thinking especially motivated by the success of *The Sound of Music*.

Columbia Studios nearly rejected *Funny Girl*, balking at the proposed budget until Stark convinced the moguls of the necessity of the nearly $10 million dollar financing. Stark defended the expenditure as only half as costly as many equivalent musicals, although the studio was obviously cautious about spending a fortune on the unknown Barbra Streisand who was untested on the widescreen. Hollywood executives could have easily feared Streisand as too large a personality for films à la Carol Channing or Ethel Merman, but the young actress came to Hollywood with a pre-sold celebrity and a guaranteed following. In addition to her concerts, New York stage plays and international recording successes, *My Name Is Barbra* had aired a month before the Rastar film contract was finalized in the spring of 1965. The performer's television triumph has been widely analyzed as a crucial precursor of her transition to cinema.

Of the three separate film contracts for rival companies which the absolute beginner brought to Hollywood-- *Funny Girl* for Columbia, *Hello, Dolly!* for Fox, *On a Clear Day* for Paramount-- Streisand has concluded, "I didn't feel they were taking a chance on me. You see, we're only ourselves. We have only ourselves to sell. And everything I'd ever done, I'd done on my own-- and it made money for someone else." Even before she filmed a frame of celluloid, it was commonly sensed in the industry and in the press that Barbra Streisand would enter the next decade as the most influential film superstar of all.

Sidney Lumet was signed as the *Funny Girl* director, and the start-date was set for March 1967. Lumet's film vision was widely opposed, to encapsulate much of the dramatic story in a nearly half-hour montage, and the director left in January due to "artistic" and "interpretative differences" with Stark (Hollywood terms always used in quotations). At the time the star herself preferred Mike Nichols and George Roy Hill to bring their project to the widescreen.

By the spring of 1967 a new director had been selected and the production was finalized as a Columbia Studios picture. After forty years in Hollywood, sixty-five films and a record eleven Academy Award nominations, with three wins, William Wyler was signed for his first musical. Stark was initially concerned that Wyler would be slow in handling a new format and that the veteran director would assume more control than the producer was willing to yield. But finally Stark agreed to Wyler's stipulation that he co-produce as well as direct, given not only a large salary but points in the box office take.

The renowned "women's director" had guided many actresses into Oscar-winning performances, and in the case of the cinema *Funny Girl*, Barbra Streisand was Fanny Brice, the creator and veteran player of the role, totalling 798 performances in two very healthy seasons on Broadway, not counting the three-month London extension. In preparation for the film, Stark asked Wyler to view the actress' West End performance in London, which convinced the director to accept. In the beginning Streisand may have thought she wanted a younger director than Wyler, with whom she was unfamiliar, but she readily agreed after seeing the film maker's memorable *Wuthering Heights* on television. She quickly realized Wyler's proven gifts, and they became friends, continuing to socialize until his death in 1981.

The director began his first musical on his sixty-fifth birthday, motivated by the new kind of musical challenge and the opportunity to direct a dazzling Streisand in her debut, capturing the performer's brilliance on the widescreen. Wyler made the picture more dramatic, dropping eight songs from the stage in lieu of the heightened emotional focus of the Arnsteins' romance, finally resolving the book's chief flaw. With Stark hoping to have another director create the musical sequences, he was surprised when Wyler independently suggested a paired strategy, so that Herb Ross was made responsible for the musical portion.

Associated with the Streisand career since he choreographed the Broadway musical *I Can Get It for You Wholesale*, stage musical veteran Herb Ross was given the important distinction of being the film's musical director. He shared the overall creation of the film with the director of the dramatic footage, William Wyler, who nonetheless supervised and influenced the musical decisions to a large extent. Of the 16 songs filmed, Wyler mostly inspired what the actress sang in character, such as "People," with Ross solely responsible for the production numbers. The two directors created the comic ballet on wheels, the unforgettable "Roller Skate Rag," which had been a casualty of the cumbersome stage production.

Veteran scriptwriter Isobel Lennart (*Love or Leave Me*) had written endless drafts of the libretto when *Funny Girl* was in tryouts in late 1963 and early 1964, and her screenplay was a fusion of the best elements from the approximately 100 versions. The film version would create even more of a Streisand showcase than the stage vehicle, both leading characters deepened by Lennart as she heightened the romance. Various elements of the Broadway production, including discarded songs, were salvaged when the musical was opened out for the widescreen. Over a dozen musical sequences would remain in the final cut, featuring one full hour of music in the 2½-hour picture.

In the transition from the famous play to the movie, the songs that were upheld included the sound and long-lasting "People," "You are Woman, I am Man," "Don't Rain on My Parade," "I'm the Greatest Star," and "If a Girl Isn't Pretty." Composer Jule Styne and lyricist Bob Merrill wrote four new songs, including the eloquent title song; "Roller Skate Rag"; an unlikely but superb "You Gotta Have a Swan" parody of "The Swan"; and Arnstein's "Locked in a Pink Velvet Jail," a.k.a. "Temporary Arrangement."

Considering the romance with Sharif, allegations were obviously untrue that Streisand would have her co-star's song cut from the film, but with the fourth song cut, the songwriters would be ineligible for an original song score Oscar nomination. Streisand was especially intrigued by one production number, then called "I Did It on Roller Skates and I Can't Wait to Do It on Skies," especially since she had not skated in years. Instead of the stage Fanny's debut song "Cornet Man" sung at Keeney's, she warbles "Roller Skate Rag" with the chorus, displaying her funny girl gifts by wildly disrupting the rolling routine.

Fanny Brice had sung "I'd Rather Be Blue Thinking of You (Than Be Happy with Somebody Else)" in the late twenties film *My Man*, and the song, with two others associated with Brice, were added to the *Funny Girl* film score. At the vaunted moment when a star is born, Fanny sings the ballad (ironically co-written by Billy Rose) in which the comedienne demonstrates her equally awesome talent as a songstress. Another Brice comic hit was "Second Hand Rose," by James Hanley and Grant Clarke, which had also not been in the *Funny Girl* stage show but would be used on film. Thirdly, Maurice Yvain's "My Man" provided a passionate finale substituting for the "Don't Rain on my Parade" reprise of the play. Although "My Man" was brilliantly delivered instead of the unforgettable song "The Music That Makes Me Dance," why not both?

Jules Styne, now in his eighties, was determined to star Frank Sinatra opposite Barbra Streisand, the singer-songwriter playing Fanny's husband Nick Arnstein. The Arnstein characterization would have been more fully realized as well, and Sinatra was interested, having been persuaded that they would add a handful of songs to make the picture less of "the girl's story," but Stark was indifferent. "Sinatra's all wrong. We need a big, attractive man. Someone with Cary Grant class." [Theodore Taylor's Styne biography]

When talk was insistent that Sinatra would balk at a subordinate role, the actress gave three reasons why she should be headlined over her co-star: she was a woman; it was her first film; he just should... Certainly the great Sinatra would have meant a more memorable musical, but it was the woman's personally beloved Omar Sharif who inspired a Streisand spectacular.

After the overage Frank Sinatra was rejected by the producer, Marlon Brando, Gregory Peck and Tony Curtis refused, for unknown reasons other than vague reluctance to be second-billed. Streisand was asked to meet and approve Sharif, having to be convinced that the actor should be her co-star, but she could hardly have liked the Egyptian more than she did, evidently attracted from her first vision. Streisand was seeking the opportunity to have a more realistic and pleasing Nick Arnstein than the stage show had afforded, and when meeting Omar Sharif, she recognized the kind of co-star she had envisioned. Their unlikely extramarital affair ignited the many gossips who delighted in what was apparently a true story.

It was a situation begging to be both magnified and painstakingly distilled in the Hollywood's media cottage industry: an extraordinarily talented Jewess with aquiline ethnic features, the last of the old-time movie stars with an unbelievable public following, filming a certain smash musical and committing adultery with an Arab sex symbol. On the set the co-stars' relationship was amiable and professional, but the press greedily tracked the many times the actor was in the woman's dressing room, and gossip columnists first hinted-- then loudly proclaimed-- the four-month affair between the stars who were married to others at the time. The Barbra Streisand & Omar Sharif experience is detailed in one of the next chapters.

One month after taping *The Belle of 14th Street* in April 1967, Streisand flew into Los Angeles International, where reporters were waiting for her arrival, the star deplaning with infant Jason in her arms and Sadie and her husband alongside. The famous quote upon meeting the press: "To me being a star is being a movie star." The actress described her trek west, an often-repeated remark: "Sure, you can be a star on Broadway or on TV. But when you think of the word `star,' you immediately think of somebody like Ava Gardner or Lana Turner." Elliott Gould could only remain for a couple of days to help his wife get settled, returning to Broadway for Jules Feiffer's satiric comedy *Little Murders*, which quickly closed. Returning to his wife, he did not have to be in New York until summer, when he was to star with Shelly Winters in a road show version of *Luv*.

During the lengthy *Funny Girl* production, Streisand paid $3,250-per-month rent for director Jean Neguleso's Beverly Hills home built years before by Greta Garbo, and the film fledgling was driven to the studio only fifteen minutes away in a chauffeured Cadillac. She enthused, "[Hollywood is] great. If you don't like great weather it's not so great. Me, I think it's fun to have an element of chance in the weather. But then I was thinking this morning that maybe that's why Hollywood is the movie capital of the world. The weather." [9-67 Glenna Syse interview/CDN]

Streisand was to rehearse the picture for 12-16 weeks and film for five months, the total production involving eight months of her life. The Hollywood newcomer received a modestly-furnished dressing room, her trailer well guarded by studio security. Preparing for her film debut, Streisand finally took voice lessons, studying with vocal coach Lee Sweetland who suggested she nurture her lyric soprano voice. They even contemplated recording an album of operatic arias.

Streisand reportedly considered plastic surgery, for the last time, when about to appear before the cameras, aware that it was then or never for a nose job: the widescreen would magnify her imperfections a hundredfold. Herb Ross directed the actress' screen test, photographed for several hours in various lights, hairstyles and makeup. He and she alike were flabbergasted by how well her unique charisma transferred to 35-millimeter celluloid, her initial anxiety gradually lessening and disappearing as she saw the results. "This is just like going to the movies, isn't it?", the thrilled young woman remarked. The musical director later remembered, "Those tests were beautiful. Garbo was special, Dietrich was special. No great star conformed to the norm. And Barbra is in that classic tradition." [Quoted 1-77 *Photoplay*]

Herb Ross had been friends with the young woman since the beginning of her career, a brother-sister relationship with which she was quite comfortable. "I was there holding her hand the first day that she saw herself onscreen... I couldn't believe how she could be so unerring in angling her face to the most flattering light. I discovered her secret: she has incredibly sensitive skin and is guided by the warmth of the light on her face." [11-12-78 *N.Y. Times*]

The actress was contracted for her Hollywood debut without a prior screen audition, all according to her own plan, having always had a self-vision of a great movie actress. Ross and the others were not so confident until a simple screen test easily displayed the woman's awesome ability to project her voice, to project power, to play with a camera, to effect a varying scene, although Ross has said they had no idea of her great impending popularity. He considered her "extremely lucky" for her first film role to have been the stage heroine she had originated and perfected over two years. The public especially lucky as well, considering that most Broadway stars are not asked to film the characterization they invented. Streisand's natural ambivalence about her film debut made her fearful that the public might not accept her as a movie star, but she ignored her insecurity.

The novice film actress deeply resented Ray Stark's publicity seeking at whatever cost or maneuver. Her animosity possibly included the splashy welcoming party he hosted at his Bel Air home, with many celebrities in attendance to welcome the new star. Streisand received a notorious bad rap for arriving ninety minutes late and leaving early, when she was actually terrified of the unfamiliar environment. But her reputation after the party was inexorably shaped as the aloof, arrogant newcomer. In reality she had changed clothing three times before finally accepting her appearance in a silver sequined dress as presentable, although she could not quell her dizziness and the nervous sickness in her stomach.

It was only anxiety about the awesome names invited to the party which made her inevitably late. Hanging onto Gould and Erlichman as she entered the outdoor event at Stark's estate, she descended the stairs and hastily sat down, then soon retreated inside. She quizzed such film greats as Cary Grant, Rosalind Russell and Natalie Wood about camera advice. The young woman awkwardly met her idol, Marlon Brando: "What are you doing here?", she asked in astonishment. The actor bent to talk to the overnight peer who sat nervously holding onto a small table. After the five-minute encounter with the hero of her teens, she and Gould left the main living room and would not return. Cloistering herself in the library, the woman was too timid to approach the major stars gathered in her honor and later apologized that she did not know what to say to them anyway, expecting Stark to bring the 300 important guests to her. When she complained, "I didn't know any pictures would be taken," someone insensitively noted, "This will give you an idea of what you're in for."

Another such public event was held by Rock Hudson, which his publicists gave for the actor's personal career promotion, and Streisand soon left the publicity stunt after she realized it was not the private gathering she had expected, balking at the presence of the press and photographers. She vehemently rejected the event hosted for Carol Burnett: "Revolting... All those photographers... I didn't know people invited photographers to parties in their own homes...." The Goulds only attended for their friend Carol Burnett's sake and stayed but briefly. [8-29-67 *Chicago Tribune*]

A frequently-related Ray Stark anecdote was his statement that he employed the two most beautiful actresses in the world-- Elizabeth Taylor and Barbra Streisand. When people objected to the latter, he insisted that her outstanding loveliness was seldom noticed by those who stopped at the nose. Wyler also told reporters, "She's no great beauty, but the appeal comes from way inside and makes her damned attractive." Barbra

Streisand's provincial Jewish princess characteristics have been considered the parody of ethnicity, her career occurring at a time when Jewishness was in vogue, in part because of her. Instead of hiding her origins, like Fanny Brice or Judy Holliday, Streisand specialized in emphasizing this image.

Cinematographer Harry Stradling: "I like the nose. You can't make Barbra look like Marilyn Monroe. But she does have a beautiful face--because she's got something back of it." The actress was enthused about the grainy look she noted in European films (from cheaper stock film) and thought it appropriate for *Funny Girl*, at least in parts. Stradling pacified her, "Okay, Barbra. I'll tell you what we'll do. I'll go ahead and shoot the picture like we usually do-- and afterwards we'll scratch up the film for your grainy look."

The actress was allowed to apply her own makeup, and she used a portable mirror with varying lightbulbs dictated by the film lighting. She was annoyed when she left the film capital during the brief visit to New York City for her Central Park concert that gossips pretended that she had also gone out of town for plastic surgery. "I look good in the rushes, and they can't take it," she griped. After having her hair cut short, she wore wigs for the role. The woman insisted upon using her own hairstylist, Fred Glaser, instead of the studio employees, which contradicted union regulations. Glaser was discovered and banned from the set, although he continued to work with the woman at her home.

From the beginning the novice actress quizzed the technicians and cameramen about movie-making details. She had brought slides with her of what had succeeded and what had failed in photographing her for television. Armed with her memory of details from every script from Broadway to Hollywood, Streisand actively contributed to the production, in many ways acting as one of the film makers, if unpaid and uncredited. Filming the opening sequence, she recalled a discarded line from the original play drafts which the others, including the writer, had forgotten; the line was rescued and judged perfect for the film. Competing with storied veterans, the Hollywood newcomer argued, "*Funny Girl* is part of my life. I felt I had a right to voice an opinion." The star's New York psychoanalyst occasionally few to Hollywood to soothe the actress' rites of passage. Many times she called Stark late at night for long calls concerning the filming.

Herb Ross requested a historical length of rehearsal time for the *Funny Girl* musical production numbers and was granted three months, rehearsals and pre-recording beginning simultaneously. The choreographer especially concentrated on the "Beautiful Bride," "The Swan" and "Roller Skate Rag" production numbers. The advance preparation was intended to introduce Streisand to a different medium as well as polishing the performances.

One intense aspect of filming the actress found pleasurable was the preparation for the "Chicken Lake Ballet," a.k.a. "The Dying Swan," a.k.a. "You Gotta Have a Swan," a.k.a. "Swan Lake." Broadway's "Rat-Tat-Tat-Tat" production number was replaced with a Hollywood musical tradition, "Swan Lake," when Stark discovered a photo of his mother-in-law in a ballet costume which inspired the scene meant to mimic elite art. A "flying" expert arranged Streisand's aerial hijinks. After three months of rehearsal and ten shooting days, the elaborate scene would be severely condensed in the final print although reinstated very successfully for the European release.

The new Hollywood star wondered why the work had to be in such laborious bits and pieces, the film medium so different that she felt they were undergoing a wholly separate project, despite her familiarity with the role. "I'm always amazed when I see anything come out good, because it seems like it can never come out good because of all the technical facets of it," she noted of the unique cinema challenge. "Making movies is easier because you can't hear the coughing of audiences, but harder because you can't hear the applause," she stressed several times. "It's not a musical musical, it's like a play with music. There are only three songs done in context-- one of Nick's and two of mine-- the rest are performances. It's nice to play an intimate scene intimately and not have to project to the balcony. I like to talk low, and on this day they even had trouble picking me up sometimes." [11-27-67 *L.A. Times*]

Streisand once recalled a particularly tiring day on the set, when she wished she could leave rehearsal early. "The musical director pointed to the chorus girls and said: `They're tired too and they're being paid a helluva lot less than you, so just get back to work.' And I did." Not having performed for nearly ten months, the singer was unhappy to learn during the rehearsals that her voice was off, not singing to her own satisfaction at least. The muscles she had previously developed in her throat and diaphragm which made it easier to sing had lessened, she felt. [8-73 Mary Kaye interview]

Musical conductor Walter Scharf analyzed the Streisand sound as "one part jazz, one part humor, one part pure drama and ten parts soul." He decided to make the musical arrangements with modern recording marvels, instead of restricting the sound to the period. The musician considered only Streisand and Al Jolson truly electrifying musical superstars, precluding Crosby, Presley and Sinatra, but when he was asked to work on two later Streisand musicals, he reportedly balked: "Once was enough."

In addition to appearing at a Rally for Israel's Survival (State of Israel Bonds) that summer, Streisand performed for 20,000 in a Hollywood Bowl concert intended as the west coast counterpart to her famous "Happening in Central Park" in June. The day following her soldout Bowl performance, the film company left for New York during the second week in July for the New Jersey location work. Attempting to have Columbia Studios film *Funny Girl* wholly in Manhattan, New York City Mayor John Lindsay negotiated with Ray Stark over shooting large portions of the musical on location, a practice then avoided because of the fears of higher costs. But most of the movie was to be filmed at the studio's soundstages then located in Hollywood near Sunset and Vine, with highlighted location shooting scheduled for the east coast.

The New York interval required the star to awaken at dawn to have as much natural light outdoors as possible, a timetable which conflicted with her ingrained theater hours. "Don't Rain on My Parade" (with Wyler supervising) required ten shooting days. The company worked from strategic visual points of New York Harbor to show Fanny onboard a tugboat as she chases after the man she loves, finally sailing majestically past the Statue of Liberty in a pivotal scene filmed at a cost over $600,000. In the film the aerial photography reveals a sweeping view of the skyline, drops to Fanny on the bridge of the tugboat, then retreats into another grand outline of the New York tableaux.

Beginning July 11 at a long-abandoned relic due to be demolished, the landmark railroad station in Jersey City, the climactic Act One finale was shot on five major locations in the New York-New Jersey area. The film makers contributed to the star quality-- audience eyes riveted on the performer-- with costumes designed to be visually appealing, such as the vivid orange dress which contrasts so well among the crowded train station, even in the distance.

Barbra Streisand's first day before motion picture cameras was July 11, stepping from the train onto the station platform on a hot and moist day. During the constant retakes for the brief scene when the Ziegfeld star is asked to pause for the photographers, Streisand suddenly improvised a comic gesture, averting her face from the train's exhaust and coughing and waving the smoke away. The film makers were enchanted with her unscripted prowess, but the star was nonplussed by all the attention. "Why should anything change just because the camera is on?  It was honest, wasn't it?  There's smoke-- you cough." [1-68 *Redbook*]

The next location site was Pier 84 on the Hudson River where a fast glimpse would show that Fanny had missed Nicky's oceanliner, the woman running down the pier singing a chorus of the upbeat song as she frantically begs a ride on the tugboat.  The same one-minute sequence of the desperate sprint was filmed over and over for an hour, until Streisand began "kvetching".  "They give me a chair with my name on it.  So when do I get to use it?", she sighed to a reporter.  The unhealthy heat was overwhelming, and the actress had to act as though it were a winter day in 1915 as she scampered down the pier clutching her wilted yellow roses from Nick, her makeup box and luggage (empty bags, at least).  Stark admonished the actress that the scene would cost tens of thousand per minute of location filming, and she pretended to be appalled, "Oh, my God, I can't act on anything so expensive, Ray.  I gotta talk to you!"

That mid-July afternoon was becoming rapidly overcast, pressuring the entire company, but Streisand was still required to repeat the thirty-yard dash wearing high heels.  Her feeble protests were half-serious, probably hoping to exert some influence over the film makers.  "You better get it right this time," she exhorted them, and after one such take, she could tell by reading their lips-- or most likely the body language-- that the scene was still wrong.  She pretended to threaten the producer, "Boy, am I gonna sue you.  My back hurts.  My feet hurt."  Pointing to her crepe wool costume, she complained, "This is wool-- W-O-O-L.  You know, from a lamb."  For the next take the star was directed to lose a few of the roses as she ran down the pier, but she moaned that the thorns pricked her fingers.  When told that the take was finally a keeper, she pitched the bouquet of flowers in the harbor, exclaiming "Wheeee!"  Before further filming at the pier, she was allowed to rest in a cabin cruiser rented as a kind of dressing room. [7-19-67 *N.Y. Times*]

A model cast as a Ziegfeld Follies Girl, Carolyn Kenmore, wrote a 1969 autobiography, *Mannequin: My Life as a Model*, claiming that she permanently lost her pleasure at being a Streisand fan after briefly working on the film. Outfitted in hot oversize fur coats and full-length dresses and huge feathered hats, she and nine other Follies Girls were to be photographed in the background of the scene in which the Ziegfeld group leaves the train. With the July temperature in the 80's worsened by the filming lights, everyone stood posed waiting for Streisand to appear at the railroad station, and they were to be left standing, as the model misrepresented the laborious filming.

On the fourth day, Streisand and her so-called retinue arrived in a limousine, where a large number of fans was also waiting to witness the event. The filming was to show Fanny and Georgia (Anne Francis) following the other Ziegfeld Girls off the train. With everyone in place, miserably hot and makeup wilting, Anne Francis could hardly bear to wait a few minutes more for Streisand to ready herself.

Kenmore envied the breeze from the black maid holding an electric fan next to the star, who was described as oblivious to the work in progress. Anne Francis' patience quickly dissipated after a few more minutes, and she threw a temper tantrum. Wyler tried to pacify the character actress, but she was ready to quit. Kenmore claimed that Streisand was eating, still heedless of the $5,000-per-minute delay. "Then the director would have to go on bended knee to her and invite her to join the party." This would-be actress also claimed that the star was cold to the cast and crew, magically transforming into Fanny's warm personality until the cameras stopped, then becoming cold again-- such an unintended testimonial to the star's acting ability. Kenmore's catty credibility must be aligned with that of Anne Francis, two woman obviously frustrated by their own careers and so transparently jealous of Streisand, who cared not at all, blissfully unaware of the animosity of an extra and a supporting player. Kenmore complained that Streisand cared nothing for the hard-working crew and film makers who were laboring on her behalf. Consider this statement: "The word was out that Miss Streisand had looked over the Ziegfeld Follies Girls and anybody she considered too pretty was getting reshuffled into the back row. I had never seen a woman so bold, so crude, so uncouth, and so unfeminine in my entire life." Perhaps if this model had not written "the word was out," this passage would not be so unbelievable.

# Chapter 19

"Fanny Brice

Is Reincarnated as Barbra Streisand"

After the New York location work wrapped in late July, the *Funny Girl* company returned to Los Angeles to rehearse the principle photography. The Fanny Brice film role had been custom made to appeal to the star's earliest fantasies, such as the "Swan Lake" routine for the would be childhood ballerina. The actress relished the filming of the widely publicized parody requiring three months of serious rehearsal and preparation, the seven minute sequence involving a week of filming all morning and afternoon. Although she had had little formal instruction before, Streisand researched dance at performances of the Royal Ballet then on tour in Los Angeles. Ross was surprised by the star's graceful dancing, and she remembered her lessons as a child: "My mother made me quit; she thought it was bad for my ankles." Although the comic number meant to mock the classic ballet, the actress effected a kind of nobility as she pirouetted about the stage, a performer so intensely involved that she had to be reminded that they were ridiculing the classic.

The ballet lover determined that the "Swan Lake" dance would be a barbed parody, hilarious but not foolish. With Streisand uncertain of the dramatic motivation, the musical director challenged the performer during rehearsal until she was able to envision scorn for an ignorant prince who would want to shoot the swans. The kooky spoof allowed the actress to give a melodramatic lift to the familiar ballet as she urged the hunters, "Go shoot a duck, a pigeon, an Indian!"

The actress invented much of the comic Yiddish dialogue, her disdain immense as her arms enveloped the swans. "Vat you gonna do? You gonna shoot dese svans? Dese lovelies? Vat are you... dumbness? You're some kind of a nut maybe? Dese beauties are mine tvinkletoes. Show him your tvinkle, sweetie. Come here, Prince." An actor flew over in a showy hop, and Fanny utters in contempt, "You had to do dat, heh? I mean, you couldn't just valk over like a poyson?" With the entire company laughing, Ross urged her not to forget the last line, which pleased the actress, joking, "Yeah, sure. What was that line again?"

Streisand was especially proud of this number, because the challenge was not just to sing but to act in song. She would feel helplessly thwarted when the brilliant production number was inexplicably condensed in the final release, a montage mixed with scenes of Arnstein's gambling as he misses his wife's latest opening.

Arising at 5:30 in the morning in an attempt to be on the set by 7:30, the hard-working actress was still rehearsing and improvising with Ross until the rest of the cast arrived at 9:00. After the three months of rehearsal and preparation, the long filming days were exhausting, and the star often soaked her aching feet in a bathtub of ice. Filming continued at the studios for a month during Los Angeles' seasonal heat wave, from mid-August to mid-September, before co-star Omar Sharif joined the production, the otherwise unavailable actor having already rehearsed on Saturdays with Streisand.

The failure of *The Belle of 14th Street*, the star's third television special, no doubt made many of the lesser people involved with *Funny Girl* happy, as well as jealous rivals in general gloating over the heretofore untouchable woman's first flop. Elliott Gould had to return to the east coast for the summer stock role in *Luv* which he had been offered. Director

William Friedkin visited the actor and offered a breakthrough film role opposite Jason Robards, Jr., in *The Night They Raided Minsky's*, which was to be filmed in New York. Streisand must have been happy and relieved that she was more able to enjoy her own success without guilt, although the man worried about the extended separations from his wife, an absence which surely only aggravated the Goulds' troubled relationship as well as spurring the Sharif romance.

Between the musical's cumbersome takes the co-stars played cards, but Sharif, an international bridge expert, later declared that women lack the concentration needed. "Their mind, it flutters." [*L.A. Herald Examiner*] Streisand also played gin rummy on the set with "constant companion" Cis Corman, who played a small role in the chorus. Working at the studio's ranch in Burbank, Streisand was uncomfortably overdressed during the opening scenes filmed during the hot weather. Later that month of September, the company moved for two days to the Warren Theatre in downtown Los Angeles, the building's interior doubling as Ziegfeld's old New Amsterdam Theatre, home of the Follies. The exteriors of the Arnsteins' Long Island mansion were shot at a Bel Air home, and the stars began recording the actual soundtrack LP for Columbia Records.

The Coney Island dance hall was minutely reproduced on Studio 16, the theater set for the filming of the "Roller Skate Rag" production number, an allusion to the celebrated play logo of upside down skates. "I thought you said you could skate," the auditioning Fanny is asked, and she retorts, "I didn't know I couldn't." Stardom is assured when the young woman realizes the audience is enrapt with her antics as well as becoming mesmerized by her vocal gift. Her timid rendition of "I'd Rather Be Blue" turns into a forceful belt, for which even the crew rewarded her with an ovation during the filming, the crucial take eventually repeated ten times.

Throughout the filming William Wyler withheld dramatic close-ups until his star was well involved with a given scene, beginning with the camera shot over her shoulder, not focusing closer until the audience would have accepted the moment. Known as a disciplinarian, Wyler actually refrained from over-directing Streisand. The relationship between director and actress was relaxed and amiable, such that she would drive the man around the lot in her own studio jeep. Wyler realized that he and she both were high-strung, and he preferred her detailed concern over the lazy actress who worried about nothing. The director grasped that a self-critical perfectionist is just as dissatisfied with others as herself.

The working relationship was actually quite benign, Wyler sometimes teasing her by turning his deaf ear to the incessant talk. With a hard-of-hearing director, the actress must have seemed even more imposing having to raise her voice. One of the Wyler-Streisand allegations was that the director left the set during an unpleasant rehearsal, leaving his assistant in charge, and the untrue legend was that the star refused to continue until Wyler himself returned. Hollywood loved to portray a surely-false story, that she sat in the director's chair, arms folded and angry, finally standing upon Wyler's arrival and announcing, "Now we will work." These are transparently phony claims attributing such unprofessional behavior to Wyler and Streis-and. The facts were that the only disagreements between them were artistic, not personal.

"You mean you can't argue with the landlord?!", she deflected the criticism about her being argumentative. The newcomer fatalistically understood the initial opposition to her film debut: "It wouldn't be natural if some people didn't react with a `What's so wonderful about her?' attitude." The film crew's inside joke: "Give her a chance, this is the first movie she's ever directed." Years later the actress remembered her trust that the director's final decisions were correct. She only mentioned her suggestions in passing, and if he disagreed, she would compromise by asking that they film both versions. She told a reporter, "I have opinions and ideas and Willie respected them and I respected him. I don't know why people make a big deal out of it. I don't know what other actresses do. Do they just sort of stand around there like mummies, get dressed, get told what to do, move here, move there? Do they do that? That can be pretty boring for the actress and the director, besides what it does or does not do for the performance.... Of course I would always do what he wanted to do. He's the director."

Author Axel Madsen devoted a chapter to *Funny Girl* in his 1973 authorized biography, *William Wyler*, based in part on an April/May 1968 *Action!* article. The actress was quoted:

"At the beginning, I guess, before we started the picture, we had the usual differences most people have. At that point, I think I knew more about *Funny Girl* than Mr. Wyler. I had played it a thousand times and had read all the reviews of all the scripts-- for the movies and the play. But once we started... well, it couldn't have been a more creative relation. I don't know what people are used to . . . well, it's just the fact that people want to make trouble. But, I mean, when two people discuss things. We tried different things and experimented and so forth. It was stimulating and fun and good things came out. And, I guess, bad things, too. But, I mean, it's the only way to work."

Wyler was certain that the screen had to give more than the stage, to a more demanding audience; more versimilitude was expected, fewer of the stage's conventions. The novice musical director was not motivated by the overwrought story and its stick-figure characters-- Streisand was his chief impetus. He told *Variety*, "Going into a song in real life is most unrealistic," which of course has always been considered the delicate stickler with musicals. Wyler believed Streisand's great talents were wide-ranging enough to seem realistic as she sang while acting, especially plausible, he believed, with the enormous feeling and emotions with which she loaded her lyrics. The director believed that her enthusiasm and experimental innovations were similar to the young Bette Davis; his star's push for excellence he regarded as his goal too.

Before all the cast and crew, Streisand had been too anxious to summon tears for an important scene filming in the late summer. When she was first required to cry after her explosive rendition of "I'm the Greatest Star," she could not feel the emotion. Although glycerine was attempted, the artificial tears were rejected. Wyler embraced her and suggested, "Barbra, take it slowly. Don't try hurrying it. Do it as you feel it." The soundstage was quiet, with a volatile suspense, everyone dreading failure. The woman expended all the passion in her soul for the essential statement song, finishing on the floor as she bawled and then bent over. She was still crying when she lifted her eyes to the audience of one, wondering of Keeney's assistant, "Do you believe me?" The director, wisely not expecting another take of the emotional outpouring, knew that the scene was perfect. "Cut and print!" He complimented his actress, "That was good, Barbra, very good."

The Wyler biography also quoted the director's observations of the star's battles with the producer and her husband's role in protecting her. "He came in and sort of straightened things out. He was very good at that." The director saw the couple's break-up as inevitable, with the plot ironically similar to *Funny Girl*'s. The situation was to him also akin to his personal problems thirty years earlier when he was still an obscure director married to a famous star, Margaret Sullivan. Streisand:

I feel we had a great sort of chemical relationship. Willy can't, um, dissect a scene for you. I mean, he would go, `Oomph, a little more oomph,' and I'd say, `Okay, I know what you mean.' And I would give it a little more oomph. A lot of people are not like that, but I couldn't have wanted a better relationship. He let me see the rushes with him, and I'm supposedly the first actress who's seen them. He knows I'm not destructive. I'm very objective about my work.

She continued to be obsessed with her acting, even during the times Wyler took her to dinner. She would discuss the next day's shooting with the script in her hands, recounting the similar scene from all of the various performances of the stage shows.

Despite the legendary number of re-takes Wyler was said to require, Streisand has clarified that these seldom numbered more than a handful. When both directors-- Wyler and Ross-- were satisfied, the actress would ask for an additional attempt and surprise the seasoned professionals with an improvement. Thinking the phrasing was wrong on "People," she was unhappy with the many versions and insisted on redoing the important song, finally satisfied with the 14th rendition... shimmering, peerless perfection. A difficult challenge for the actress was the little familiar technique of lipsynching, prerecording the vocal performance and trying to match the sound with a suitable visual. The intimate filming of "People" was so frustrating to lipsynch that only the reverse finally succeeded, filming the scene followed by the overdubbing.

The actress meant to thwart the lipsynching complications by filming the climactic "My Man" close-up live, then a daring and rarely attempted technique which affords the performer no protection-- one has to give it one's all during the actual filming effort. Streisand had disliked the sterile perfection of the pre-recorded rendition: "It was too musical, too commercial, too perfect. It needed to be more dramatic." She was certain the scene should be filmed live, the film makers eventually agreeing, especially that beginning as a close-up instead of a long shot facilitated the live technique captured in one continuous filming. [*L.A. Times*]

Although the fact of a woman's influencing a major film production was alien to the crew, the director appreciated the promise of filming live. The effect was total realism, creating an extemporaneous performance far superior to the usual Hollywood musical which often fails to match the lips to the sound. Wyler suggested the neutral black background of the dark drapery, inspired by Fanny Brice's original stage setting forty years earlier, and with stunning results Streisand delivered.

The well-known story is that the actress wanted Sharif in her presence, just out of the camera range, to inspire her performance (the opposite reaction for *Clear Day*'s similar scene some months later). So that she would be properly motivated before singing the finale, Streisand asked her co-star to come from the hotel, where he was packing to leave, to repeat their moving farewell dialogue after Arnstein has come from jail. He apologizes.

"I never gave you anything."

"Yes, you gave me a lot. You gave me a blue marble egg-- and you also made me feel beautiful."

"You are beautiful."

The dialogue must have reminded her of both men in her life, as it was Gould who had given her the original gift which had been written into the playscript.

A dozen takes were filmed, the actress insisting from the first moment of perfection that she could exceed herself. The song was already associated with Streisand as well as Brice, the Streisand single having been released from the *My Name Is Barbra* television soundtrack. The risky gamble of live filming would succeed in leaving the majority of critics and fans alike limp with vicariously spent emotion, the magnificent finale creating a lasting image as the audiences left the theater.

It was unfortunate that the press' pre-conceived image of a tumultuous performer was perpetuated in the ongoing coverage of *Funny Girl*. She very much resented the corporate portrayal of Barbra Streisand as a tyrant, that the public relations office capitalized upon the negative press, which was incidentally free, to develop the public's anticipation to see the picture. With the film not due to open for eighteen months, any publicity generated from the beginning was considered welcome, until Wyler protested the false image, noting that her disagreements were actually with Stark. "She's not easy, but she's difficult in the best sense of the world-- the same way I'm difficult."

In retrospect, he explained, "Some news hen didn't get the bowing and scraping she thought she deserved, and this girl got a bad press." [Lawrence DeVine interview/*L.A. Herald Examiner*]

Years later at William Wyler's March 9, 1976 Life Achievement Award ceremony at the American Film Institute, the actress noted that he would be surprised that she was only going to speak briefly in testimonial to her beloved "Willie": "It's nice to know the American Film Institution is honoring an American film institution." Nearly twenty years after *Funny Girl*, the late director's daughter created a documentary, *Directed by William Wyler*, in which Streisand also discussed her first film director, remembering that she meant to please Wyler, meaning for him to like her as well. "He would ruin a lot of takes-- he'd smoke and cough. The smoke would get in front of the lens."

Streisand recollected after *A Star Is Born* was due to open that it had become a "shopworn" cliché that she directs her directors, even as far back as her first film when it was her opinions which had made trouble. When *Funny Girl* was to become a motion picture, she had had a definite conception of the role because she had created it and was so naturally familiar with it. She would piecemeal the near dozen scripts into the best portrayal possible and knew that Wyler was grateful for her participation. The experience with him was very enjoyable: "I always had a sense of his watching me like a really fine, dear mirror."

She also recalled cameraman Harry Stradling as another true professional. "Anybody who is really a pro and talented appreciates other talent; it's only the mediocre who are threatened." Streisand emphasized that she and Stradling had had "total mutual respect" and that press reports that she was ordering him how to photograph her and that he became angry with her were untrue. [11-76 *Ladies's Home Journal*]

Journalists have doubted the cinematographer's own claims that he did not lose his temper and walk off the set on two occasions as was reported. He was admittedly chagrined the most that the fledgling actress was so often right. At first startled and then bemused by hearing her advice, he quickly accepted the woman's involvement when her instincts proved sound. Notwithstanding rumors of their incompatibility, after the actress' film debut she requested Stradling for her subsequent pictures, until he died during *Owl and the Pussycat*.

During the *Funny Girl* filming, the actress was made particularly uncommunicative and upset by the press' mishandling of her: the misquotes, the distortions, the misunderstandings. The anti-Streisand gossip grew so intense that later in the filming she feared to talk to the cast and crew lest repercussions be started, no matter that she was then damned as cool and aloof. The problem was compounded by studio personnel who leaked negative publicity in an attempt to restrain the tempestuous star.

Journalists were ruthless in portraying the Hollywood newcomer as harshly as would still sound plausible. Gossip writer Joyce Haber picked at Streisand on an ongoing basis, alleging many questionable and some patently false troubles about the production. We must accept that her accounts of the filming adroitly mixed fact and fabrication. One plausible version was how amusing all the confrontations were to the principles in retrospect, such as the star's tape made for the cast's surprise party for Stark. Streisand sang a spoof of "My Man" written by a staffer: "Oh Ray, I love him so/If some footage I can't see/I say, `Oh Gee/So What?' " The lyrics referred to the occasion when the actress became angry over the producer's reluctance to show the previous day's rushes when she had arrived especially late.

Joyce Haber wrote in *New York* magazine: "The question is, was Barbra really a bitch during her recently completed filming of `Funny Girl'?" Her surmise was that the actress was "a full-fledged girl monster." This outsider's analysis was that the star dominated the film-making, altering the dialogue and imperiously treating the director like "a butler" during the times when they were not actually fighting. The catty columnist claimed that Streisand had stalked off the set when disturbed. It is safe for us to assume that Streisand has virtually never walked off a set, for not only is such behavior beneath a practiced professional, but it is alien to the fight-not-flight personality of Barbra Streisand.

After Dorothy Manners first interviewed the star on the Columbia set, the actress wrote a two-page letter acknowledging the columnist's kindness and fair portrayal. Streisand believed that worse than her false early-career kook image was the much more inaccurate representation of a Hollywood prima donna.

"Don't believe anything you read about me," she urged. Although the star was slandered as ostentatious, cruel and cheap, reality has shown that she was gentle and very giving in her generosity, although some crew members of the time conceded that she was seldom prompt and that she had problems making small talk. Co-star Kay Medford blamed peoples' antagonism on sheer jealousy of the star's success. [4-69 *Good Housekeeping*]

Ray Stark defended his star, "The only thing she hasn't learned is tact." [10-15-68 *Look*] He excused her frequent tardiness by explaining that she lacked any sense of time, the producer claiming to disregard the delays, because with a disciplined professional who seldom wasted film, as much as two hours' time was gained by the end of the day. Stark said his star possessed not only acting ability but the rare talent to convey the truth. "She has a basic truth within herself that can stand the miserable analysis of being amplified 500 times on the big screen." [1-12-69 *London Times*] Although his star aggressively pushed for her ideas, eventually all concerned were pleased because she was maddeningly correct, which became a refrain about the junior director. The producer understood her obsessive worrying about her appearance because the widescreen was so much larger than the tiny television screen on which the world was accustomed to seeing her.

Filming ended early December at the studio, *Funny Girl* finally "in the can" a couple of weeks behind schedule but more than a million dollars under the ten million dollar budget. At the farewell party for the cast and crew, Streisand gifted all with copies of her albums as well as gold *Funny Girl* charms inscribed, "From Barbra with gratitude and deep affection." She gave Wyler an antique eighteenth century gold watch inscribed, "To make up for lost time," although a decade-and-a-half later, when asked about the gift during the *Yentl* promotion, she looked puzzled and wondered, "Did I do that?"

Wyler's wrap-up gift to Streisand was a silver director's megaphone inscribed "D.G.A." (for Director's Guild of America), a smiling credit of her enthusiasm for the total cinematic production, and also a collapsible wand. According to his biographer Axel Madsen, Wyler was just slightly jealous as he explained the gift of the conducting baton. "She pays the keenest attention to the orchestration and the playback. She has a very keen ear." Accepting the gifts, the actress said, "He wants me to go on scoring." One of Ray Stark's gifts was a ten-minute *Funny Girl* preview with the credits facetiously altered to read, "Written, Produced and Directed by Barbra Streisand."

The actress returned to her husband in New York a few days after wrapping the musical, Sharif having left several days earlier. Originally Streisand would have begun production on the Paramount musical *On a Clear Day*, but complex negotiations resulted in the delay. Late in the year Stark filed the suit to prevent his actress from working for any other employer, the dispute finally settled out of court some months later. Stark apparently withdrew his lawsuit when it failed to preclude the rival studio work and when he needed harmonious relations in order to promote *Funny Girl*. He even gave the actress a percentage in the box office, although only a scant token.

Anne Francis, who played a Ziegfeld showgirl, gave an interview about the "nightmare" experience to the *Hollywood Reporter* after the filming was completed. She failed to convince the studio to remove her name from the credits, claiming that the star had had her work cut from "three very good scenes and a lot of other ones, to two minutes of voice-over in a New Jersey railroad station." According to this bitter woman, Streisand viewed the rushes on a daily basis and cut her competitor's footage or someone else's.

"Barbra ran the whole show-- Ray Stark, Willie Wyler, Herb Ross. She had the Ziegfeld Girls scenes changed-- one day she told Wyler to move a girl standing next to her because she was too pretty, and the girl wound up in the background. Eventually, the Ziegfeld Girls scenes were eliminated altogether.... It was like an experience out of *Gaslight*. There was an unreality about it."

How silly for the rather unknown Miss Francis to claim that the Ziegfeld Girls scenes were cut, as important an aspect as they were to the film. The beauties were even beautified in a *Playboy* pictorial "The Girls of Funny Girl," only Miss Francis not undressed. If it were true that Streisand thought another woman's looks outshone her own, surely she would not admit such a fear. With a large axe to grind, Anne Francis wanted the world to see the superstar as so insecure that she feared a tiny supporting role would steal the show from her. What is so incredible is that Anne Francis was so secure that she believed she could steal the show herself.... In her 1982 autobiography, she noticeably does not even mention the incident.

Kay Medford did not complain when her third-billed role was necessarily shortened, and she still received an Oscar nomination. After Anne Francis' publicity-seeking stunt, Stark clarified to Joyce Haber that the role had been eliminated from the stage play after Boston, to shrink the musical to size. When the film version ran over three hours, the footage had to be reduced to a more manageable 2½ hours. How the character actress learned of the omission is unknown, but the producer noted that her scene had been intact only three weeks before the controversy began, in late December when Streisand had been long gone.

Columbia Studios refused to acknowledge Anne Francis' stunt, the producer retaining her film credit. Afterwards, Francis admitted being a sore loser. She was to portray Fanny's alcoholic friend, showing Fanny's compassion even when she was a big star. This scene was eliminated except for "a view of my back on a couch" as well as her singing of "Sadie, Sadie" and the Follies songs. [1-12-68 *HWD. Reporter*]

Anne Francis' allegations became the focus of an enduring anti-Streisand legend. It is ironic that the woman who played the same part Georgia James on the road with the stage original, retiring gracefully when it became necessary to trim the unwieldy musical, was later given a role in *The Way We*

*Were*, playing one of the Hollywood activists.  Streisand's version:

> "They talk about stars trying to cut someone good out of a picture.  It's a false star idea.  Anything that's good will always remain in a picture, anything bad will be cut out." [12-20-70 *L.A. Herald Examiner*]

A much later complaint:

> "I didn't have any control in `Funny Girl.'  There was a girl in it, I can't remember her name, but she went on TV and said I cut her out of the movie because she was too pretty.  And I thought, `You idiot, even if I wanted to cut you out I couldn't have.'" [11-13-83 *Herald Examiner*]

# Chapter 20

"A Jewess' Love Affair
with Hollywood's Arab Heartthrob"

Omar Sharif's autobiography recalls that when filming the 1967 Columbia western *McKenna's Gold*, he overheard Ray Stark and William Wyler discussing their upcoming *Funny Girl* project day after day in the studio commissary. The film makers were seeking a male lead which the actor described as a tough-to-cast "straight man" to the featured star. He knew that Nick Arnstein had to cue the comedienne and be attractive and still appear comfortable outfitted in a tuxedo. People were jokingly suggesting that the Egyptian actor play the very Jewish Arnstein. At one point the director asked aloud, "Well, why not Omar Sharif, anyway?"

Said to have been uncertain about the Arab alliance, the actress asked to meet Sharif. "In America, you are the woman I have most wanted to meet," the actor greeted her, overwhelming the young woman with charm and almost irresistible sex appeal, kissing her hand in the old-fashioned manner. And so Omar Sharif came to be cast opposite Barbra Streisand in *Funny Girl*.

When shooting finally commenced only days before the Israeli-Egyptian Six-Day War, an annoying notoriety would be aroused with the pairing of a Jewess with the only international Egyptian movie star (Syrian by descent, Egyptian-born and raised), and Sharif was expected to be replaced. Not only was the Jewish film with a Jewish star being financed by Jews in a pro-Israeli studio, but the press was sympathetic to the tiny Middle East nation. The Sharif scandal was caused by the realization that the actor was an Egyptian dating from the Nasser presidency, an unforeseen problem causing hysteria on the set, with the producer considering a cancellation of the actor's contract and Streisand's mother proclaiming, "My daughter isn't going to work with an Egyptian!"

Himself a Jew, Wyler protested the hypocrisy of a Democratic country discriminating against an Arab, stating that without Sharif he would quit. "Arabs and Jews have gotten along for centuries, until 20 years ago anyway. Why not in my picture?" [Lawrence DeVine interview *L.A. Herald Examiner*]

The mad excitement continued until Israel won the confrontation a few days later. Some studio personnel wanted the actor's official condemnation of his homeland; but the director again intervened. Streisand announced, "We people of the theater don't think of ourselves by race or creed. We have our own standards of judging each other--and that's talent." Reacting to the gossip that she meant to have her co-star fired, she denounced the groundless allegations as complete nonsense and asked that the "cosmopolitan" professional not even be categorized as an Arab. "The biggest reason for that outbreak among my people and his was hatred. Nothing real has been solved by rage and bitterness. My feelings toward Omar are ones of affection and admiration, and I'm sure he feels the same toward me."

A publicist was assigned to monitor the actor's media relations, and the production progressed with no further difficulties, until worldwide repercussions resulted from the first romantic scene between the Arab and the Jewess.

First a kissing picture was published in an east coast newspaper, then reprinted in Cairo where a press vendetta barraged the country in an attempt to cancel the actor's citizenship. Sharif was vilified as having betrayed Egypt by kissing a performer who had given an Israeli benefit. The actor noted that the reporters were ignorant of the context of *Funny Girl* yet labeled it pro-Israeli anyway, just in case.

When the Associated Press called Sharif for his reaction, his widely-reprinted response was, "I don't make a point of asking a girl her nationality, her occupation, or her religion before kissing her--either on the screen or off."

The funny girl's quip was similarly reported all over the world: "You think the Egyptians are angry? You should see the letter I got from my Aunt Rose." Sharif was impressed by her spontaneous fiction, but he was serious.

The actor had no problems working with the stormy performer, not when he easily understood that her bleak background had only naturally made Streisand insecure. The man admitted he saw only the star's nose at their first meeting, also being rather intimidated by her strength. An oft-repeated observation: "The first impression is that she's not very pretty. But after three days, I am honest, I found her physically beautiful, and I started lusting after this woman." [10-16-67 *Life Atlantic*]

Initially Streisand would only comment obliquely when asked about her co-star, "He's a very unique person," and would then change the subject. She later lamented, as she has been quoted, "I don't like lies told about me, and the press, when I first got to Hollywood, created all sorts of tales. They had Omar and me in bed every night of the week. If we had done that, *Funny Girl* would have never been made."

Another frequently-repeated statement, from Streisand, rather benign but quoted out-of-context, was her comment to a reporter:

> It got so I couldn't wait to get on the set in the morning. The day I knew I was going to work with Omar were happy days. The days he didn't have to work were miserable. I know Omar knew I was going `ga-ga' over him but he was too much of a

gentleman to make a play for a married woman. I would read in the columns where he took this girl and that girl out. It used to make me feel actually sick. I fell hopelessly-- madly-- in love with my leading man. It sounds like the old Hollywood story-- a B-movie script-- but it actually happened. And I don't care who knows it. I loved every second of it. [*WWD*]

The *Funny Girl* actress portrayed Fanny Brice's plainness as being only a myth-- the character's self-perception about her appearance is merely a mocking irony, and Omar Sharif as a man was certainly attracted to Barbra Streisand as a woman. "I was married, and so was she, which made the glamour more intense." They lost their heads, but when together again for *Funny Lady* the nostalgia was sweet. "Without the passion, but also without the discomfort and uncertainty." [Quoted by George Hadley-Garcia/*Barbra Now & Then* #3]

Rather than being isolated or incommunicado as the Hollywood beginner was often depicted, Streisand was in her dressing room working on her characterization and visiting with her son. Perhaps by necessity she hid a damaging column notice: "Shortly after her liaison with Omar Sharif, Gould, Barbra Streisand's husband, flew back to New York, the star and co-star of *Funny Girl*, Barbra and Omar Sharif, were seen dining together and once, it was reported, they shared dinner in his hotel suite." James Bacon even noted the name and year of the 1959 Dom Perignon champagne they consumed, writing that she told her husband, "We were going over the script."

Separated from his Egyptian wife at the time, the *Funny Girl* leading man made his Italian specialties for his friend and showed her how to play cards, she making TV dinners and helping him with his singing. They first appeared in public in mid-November at designer Courreges' fashion party at The Factory discotheque in Hollywood, which upset the woman's husband. When the press pounced on the outing, noting that Gould had been forced to remain on the east coast with his own filming, the actor told columnist Sheilah Graham in December 1967, "I'm furious with Barbra and have told her that. She should have known that she is in a very difficult position out there where the press doesn't like her because she's been uncooperative. I am a very secure person but as a man I have certain reactions. But I am furious with my wife for putting herself in this kind of position. She's a naive little girl but I love her and I know everything will work out." The aggrieved husband also called their mutual friend, Arthur Laurents, to commiserate about his wife's behavior.

Streisand's version was that she had read about the fashion show and indicated to Sharif her desire to attend, the actor holding two tickets and willing to escort her if Gould did not object. She told the press that she explained that her husband would appreciate it and that he understood. She also remarked that she had defended herself, arguing that the tickets cost $250 each. After having become visible, Streisand and Sharif were then spotted publicly again, at a fashionable Hollywood restaurant.

After their affair ended, Streisand would only describe her co-star as unforgettable, grateful to him for helping her transfer her Fanny Brice role to celluloid. But Omar Sharif once recalled on a television show that he is unable to dampen his emotion when the actors' love scene has ended. "Something lingers on. With Barbra Streisand on `Funny Girl,' it was different because I was in love with her, I really was. And it was one-sided, yet I did love her a lot. She had a lot of affection for me, but it just didn't go beyond that." He remarked elsewhere, "I am sorry to become involved in the breakup of any home, especially when there is a baby involved. But people do fall in love no matter what the circumstances and, sadly, no matter what the consequences." [Quoted 10-70 *Pageant*]

The actress returned to her husband when the filming ended, Sharif working overseas on another film and soon divorcing his wife. Streisand briefly vacationed with Elliott and Jason, then began working on her second picture. Sharif visited during her lunch hour in the isolated 20th Century dressing room, he preparing to film *Che* at the studio where she was filming *Hello, Dolly!* Hoping their marriage would survive, possibly Gould had forgiven what he believed was only a passing dalliance, and indeed no hint of extramarital romance was reported during the lengthy involvement with *Hello, Dolly!*-- but the columnists had been hinting about a troubled marriage when the Goulds officially separated in February 1969.

As the years passed, Sharif did not deny the romantic rumors concerning his *Funny Girl* co-star but insisted that their relationship be termed a "romance" and not an affair. His memoirs describe the two most memorable women in his life as actresses Barbra Streisand and Anouk Aimee. His personal antidote to the ugliness of life is love, and he admitted that the sexual act means more to him than his loverboy image projects. The actor refuted his reputation of being contemptuous toward women as he unabashedly idolizes the opposite sex. Although he knew he has never remained for long with one woman, each relationship aroused beautiful feelings of love as well as passion, which "purifies" him. He cannot bear to be openly opposed by women, he explained, although he believes men are normally proud and haughty, thus able to contradict their partners.

Although supportive of certain rights feminists have gained, the actor is only preoccupied with the females whom he encounters: "I try to get to know them and to go to bed with them." He credited his sexual success to giving himself wholly to his partner. "And I make women happy, with the tenderness, love, and thrills I give them." The intelligent, feminine women he has pursued are those who display a distinct need for him, no matter how independent they may be otherwise. He portrayed Barbra Streisand as one woman who never attempted a mental contest with him, an extraordinary romantic adventure he will never forget.

Although Streisand would have too much dignity to kiss-and-tell, detailing confidences being repugnant to her, Omar Sharif ungallantly published his candid memoirs *The Eternal Male* with a Paris firm stipulating that the writing focus on his affair with the actress. Streisand has scarcely discussed their relationship, and he was rather ungentlemanly to reveal such private events. The above portrayal is presented to form a background of a man to whom Streisand could be attracted-- it is evident that not only is the actress' image as a ballbreaker false, she was actually drawn to the subdued role of the old-fashioned woman. Her growth as a woman is seen in growing apart from this kind of man.

"Barbra Streisand, who struck me as being ugly at first, gradually cast her spell over me. I fell madly in love with her talent and her personality. The feeling was mutual for four months-- the time it took to shoot the picture," the actor observing that such temporary romances during filming are typical. "Barbra's villa served as our trysting place," not at his home where his family lived. Although insurance provisions in their contracts forbade any trips, together or apart, the couple were together in the evenings and on weekends.

"Nobody could be more conventional, more discreet than a pair of lovers. That's something for prudes to think about." They prepared their own meals, Sharif going through all the Italian pasta delights he knew, Streisand heating TV dinners. They ate these quite basic meals and watched television, rarely leaving to dine elsewhere. The first such occasion was when the actor was invited to dinner at a good friend's home, Gregory Peck. Asking whether he "could bring somebody with me," Sharif trusted his friend not to reveal their relationship, not even to a single member of the press, which he knew would terminate their short-lived liaison.

He wistfully concluded, "The years have gone by and I say to myself that Fanny Brice loved the hero of the movie, that she didn't love Omar Sharif, that I loved the heroine... that I didn't love Barbra Streisand." This illusive-love phenomenon Sharif regards as quite frequent, fantasy being more intriguing than reality, especially difficult for him as a man to halt the amorous feelings he must display to his co-star. "You see, I'm in love because I'm available and sentimental. Because I'm in love with love."

The actor later blamed the book's translator for making the intimate passages spicier than he had originally dictated. "The choice of words in some cases are not choices I personally would have made." [12-13-77 *L.A. Times*] Sharif did complain once to Rex Reed about being upstaged, "She's a monster. I had nothing to do but stand around. But she's a fascinating monster. Sometimes I just stood on the sidelines and watched her. I think her biggest problem is that she wants to be a woman and she wants to be beautiful and she is neither."

# Chapter 21

"A Superstar is Reborn

in Hollywood's *Funny Girl*"

Although Barbra Streisand was selected to present the best song Oscar in 1968-- announcing the winner as Leslie Bricusse for "Talk to the Animals" with Sammy Davis, Jr., accepting-- the actress was still not a film star, having not yet released a minute's worth of *Funny Girl*.  Ironically, a rift had developed between Streisand and Davis which baffled the black Jewish entertainer for some time.  Streisand had been the first major star to be expelled from The Factory, a chic Hollywood private discotheque, although co-founder and board member Sammy Davis, Jr., claimed he was unaware of the action taken toward Streisand when he was out of town performing.

The entertainer told columnist James Bacon, "Barbra and I always were good friends until the Academy Awards in April. Leslie Bricusse won the Oscar for the best song.  He asked me to accept and Barbra was the presenter.  Other than hand me the Oscar, she would have nothing to do with me.  All of the photographers and press noticed the coolness but I couldn't tell them anything."  It was The Factory's practice not to discuss the ejection, although it was learned that Davis truly had not been consulted.  Sitting on the Board of Directors at the time, surely he could have either rectified the unexplained action or at least personally notified Streisand of his non-involvement.

With a 155-minute running time, *Funny Girl* is still Barbra Streisand's longest picture, despite the film-makers' cuts, and carried a general audience rating. Stark suggested that six more minutes be trimmed from the weighty second half after the picture's June 1968 sneak preview; the necessary editing to the too-long footage hurt all concerned, even Streisand's favorite sequence being nearly omitted, the thirteen-minute "Swan Lake" ballet. With the planned two-and-a-half-hour running time, an intermission was included, standard for road show musicals of the time. Just following the picture's release, the actress futilely attempted to have the producer restore the entire "Swan Lake" parody to the print.

The very first ad for the movie had been in the *New York Times* on July 9, 1967, just before filming commenced, the announcement including a coupon for tickets to the world premiere in September 1968. Reservations for the road show were offered fourteen months in advance, 7,800 requests received from the ad alone and tickets continuing to be sold by mail order for six months. The musical opened with the largest pre-sold box office in history, coming to the screens with $2 million in advance tickets already guaranteed. The studio spent $1.6 million dollars on the promotional campaign, including *Funny Girl* wristwatchs alike the famous Mickey Mouse timepiece, very valuable collector's items today. The star complained in vain that certain of the advertising lines were "vulgar," possibly referring to the line "Funny that he should happen to her!"

Streisand's first reaction to the finished product was that she liked most of the picture, recognizing that if it was corny, life is corny. She told a reporter, "And on the other hand, it is a very entertaining picture. I feel people get involved with it; it's an audience picture. People seem to like it, but I wouldn't want to have to be a critic reviewing it." She wrote a congratulatory letter to the film's arranger, Walter Scharf, in August 1968. Her letter was later reproduced in industry trades as an Oscar nomination acknowledgment: "I have just seen the scored version of `Funny Girl' and I had to tell you how beautifully sensitive your music is. There were many scenes which made me cry, and honestly I couldn't tell whether it was the scene itself or your wonderful music."

That summer the producer refused to sneak-preview the show in California, knowing the many Hollywood celebrities present would offset the gauge of a "typical audience" response. Advance showings lured tens of thousands of ticket buyers for the musical sneak-previewed in Milwaukee and Dallas, with broad hints as to the identity of the film. To measure a general public reaction, out-of-the-way locales were also chosen for their scarce Jewish populations. Four of Stark's tape recorders registered only entranced silence, not the uncomfortable squirming, coughing and giggling he had feared.

Toronto's *Daily Star* triggered a diplomatic confrontation with the studio when the newspaper's critic attended the Milwaukee showing, discreetly sitting in the audience. The review related the decidely non-ethnic Wisconsin audience tremendously applauding each song. Even though his critique was a rave, the studio wanted to keep the picture under wraps until its official September premiere, fruitlessly imploring him not to violate precedent and ethics with the premature coverage.

The $100-per-ticket premiere of the $8.8-million Technicolor/Panavision road show musical was held at Broadway's Criterion Theatre on Wednesday, September 18, 1968, the proceeds benefitting New York Mayor Lindsay's Commission on Youth and Physical Fitness. Streisand blurted that she had never worked with benefits as a youth: "I was always up for charity myself. I could have used some help." Bedecked in a directoire hairstyle wig, the actress wore a sheer silver-net gown covered with jeweled spider web designs. The Arnold Scaasi creation had been delivered that day and was nearly demolished by 21-month-old Jason's chalk and crayon drawings.

The New York world premiere was considered a local, national and international news event, live television cameras covering the glittery premiere which began 45 minutes late due to snarled foot and auto traffic. Streisand later remembered her first of many such premieres, "It was so exciting to go to an opening night and not be nervous and have to worry. I always envied my friends the fact that they could get dressed up and go to my openings while I had to worry and work. Now, I can go to the theater and watch myself work."

She was less concerned than usual about her appearance, knowing it was the onscreen presentation which was most crucial. Perhaps unavoidably, memories of her many hours spent as a youth at Loew's Kings Theater occasionally interrupted her reverie. Her confidence and mood soared when the theatergoers applauded every number, and at the no-holds-barred ending, the stunned audience momentarily paused, the patrons then applauding Streisand with an explosive standing ovation. This immediate silence was to be a universal occurrence, and Stark admitted that he had panicked the first time it happened in Wisconsin.

The after-theater tent party on Times Square began at 11:00 p.m., gathered fans offered a three-way view through the transparent plastic sides. With the traffic temporarily halted, a cordon of police protected the star and her husband as they crossed the street on a red carpet to the vacant lot behind Shubert Alley where the massive tent was erected for the block party. Streisand and her husband sat with members of her family, as well as hobnobbing with Mayor John Lindsay, the master of ceremonies who greeted the triumphant actress, "It's a long way from Brooklyn to Broadway." Her celebrated retort, "It's not so long if you take the BMT and change at Canal Street." She declared that this first film star premiere made her feel like a "kid with a play thing." The Goulds drank only soft drinks amid all the liquor, the star announcing, "It's the only thing I like." The couple did not remain as long as expected, possibly unnerved by the mob of fans staring at the star.

Hollywood may have forecast the film's failure, even wished it so, but *Funny Girl* was a blockbuster hit, an all-time Top Twenty box office record for years, the excess of $50 million dollars at the box office a record sum in the late sixties. At the studio's unprecedented $6.00 price, reserved seat engagements played at showcase theaters for over a year before *Funny Girl* was widely released. With Hollywood musicals a threatened genre, *Funny Girl* reversed the failing box office trend represented by such films as *Star!*

A few weeks after the New York premiere when Streisand arrived in Los Angeles for the west coast opening, her husband had preceded her one day earlier for *Bob & Carol & Ted & Alice* rehearsals. The actor's wife had forgotten to bring his dinner jacket, and it was flown to California by express air for the October 9th event aiding the Cedars-Sinai Hospital. The Egyptian Theater's 1,000 guests partied across the street in a tent decorated as a 1920's Lower East Side block party; among the numerous celebrities was Diana Ross.

Jack Benny greeted Streisand and said that he had left his bedside to see her succeed in her film. The $125,000 raised for charity was $25,000 more than expected, the most generous premiere donation in Hollywood history, with eighteen other national openings donating to other charities as well. Unlike her timid attendance at the New York premiere, Streisand lingered at the west coast celebration until 1:00 a.m. Having been rumored as pregnant, the actress opened her white coat to show her slim waistline and laughed, "I'm not that lucky."

Some days later, in early November, Mayor Joseph Alioto hosted the first annual San Francisco Film Festival's Samuel Goldwyn Award ceremonies honoring *Funny Girl* as the "Best American Motion Picture of 1968," and Streisand, Stark and the others flew to the Bay City to accept the honor. With the director absent, the producer and star joked about who truly directed *Funny Girl*, and Streisand graciously accepted the award from the mayor. When she and Sidney Poitier received "Star of the Year" awards from the National Association of Theater Owners in late November, also in San Francisco, she declared, "It's great to be on the same platform with Sidney Poitier. Ray originally wanted to use Sidney for Nick Arnstein in *Funny Girl*, but we decided he looked too Jewish. So we went in another direction!"

Before flying to London a few months later for the first of *Funny Girl*'s foreign openings, the actress taped a fairly detailed BBC-TV promotional interview with Michael Dean in her rented home. The day prior to the January 1969 British premiere she held a two-hour press conference at the Dorchester Hotel and explained to one inquisitive reporter that Gould was at home with their young son, the husband also committed to filming. She dismissed the Omar Sharif rumors as "ridiculous, malicious gossip" and to this day has not discussed their relationship. Ray Stark shipped by air express ten pounds of hot dogs as a prank, which prompted the actress to wake the producer late at night his time, asking only "So where's the mustard?", before breaking the transatlantic connection.

The London premiere "in the Gracious Presence of H.R.H. The Princess Margaret, President of the Invalid Children's Aid Association" drew worldwide attention. Not for the first time, the royal hostess unnerved Barbra Streisand, but seeing that the star was tongue-tied, her escort Omar Sharif intervened. "I see that your co-star is helping you out again," the princess laughed. Streisand asked reporters later, "What could I say? Everything seemed like a cliché. But the whole evening was a dream. The British certainly know how to put on a premiere." [1-21-69 *WWD. Reporter*]

A gala party was held at Claridge's, the orchestra playing the National Anthem to mark the arrival of the princess. "People" was then heard, inviting Streisand to lead the procession of guests into the main ballroom, and Princess Margaret cheerfully encouraged the actress, "I think you ought to go in, dear, they're playing your tune." The actress met a very special person at the party, Canadian Prime Minister Pierre Trudeau.

In his memoirs *I Remember It Well*, French actor Maurice Chevalier recounted the occasion when he was asked to escort the American actress to the Paris opening. They had met during her Broadway days, and he looked forward to the event. "The young Jewess who looked pretty much the way nature made her when I met her on Broadway had turned herself into a Hollywood superstar." They had to circle the block once while they waited for the crowds to dissipate, and then the photographers fell over themselves to capture the two legends on film.

Reporters also recounted the frenzied commotion, twenty-five minutes elapsing before the stars surmounted the noisy ambushing crowd of 150 photographers from five countries, climbing the many steps to reach their seats. The paparazzi broke the police lines and stormed the Opera House, continuing to snap pictures in the dark even after the picture was screening. Although the legendary hall was dark, spotlights outlined Streisand and Chevalier as they walked to their seats next to Omar Sharif, with whom the woman passed much of the evening in conversation while her official escort watched the picture. Chevalier recognized that Streisand's graciousness in greeting all the famous people disguised her extreme nervousness. "Judaism's loveliest flower had captivated the hearts of Paris...." At the film's conclusion a golden spotlight shone on the star's seat as she received a standing ovation.

Streisand stayed at the residence of Ambassador Sargent Shriver and his wife, Eunice Kennedy. Important politicians and celebrities gathered for the festivities honoring the French premiere, such as the great Maria Callas who described Streisand as the only non-operatic singer who ever received a standing ovation at the Opera House. At intermission, the late diva had joined Streisand, Chevalier and Sharif for a quartet picture. With the star then shooting *On a Clear Day*, the orchestra at the dinner party played the Lerner-Lowe score in addition to the *Funny Girl* music. Streisand sang "My Man" (originally a French standard) at a party and was moved to tears by the enrapt reception.

*Funny Girl* became a hit in foreign markets where musicals generally do not fare so well. Thomas Quinn Curtiss in *International Herald Tribune* noted that modern musicals were simply not popular with the French, even films which had triumphed elsewhere. "It was an audacious move, then, to give the film version of the Broadway musical, *Funny Girl*, its continental premiere at the Opera. This was certainly a bold thrust at the stubborn opposition, and apparently it was a victorious blow!"

After *Funny Girl* played continuously at the Criterion in New York and the Egyptian in Hollywood for one year, Columbia Studios celebrated with a special east coast benefit screening and dinner party, when Streisand cut a seven-foot birthday cake. *Funny Girl* was still drawing crowds three months later when *Hello, Dolly!* opened, the first picture only then receiving wider general distribution.

According to the trades, a contract clause stipulated that Streisand had had the option to sing the *Funny Girl* title song and/or score in German, Italian and French, but the foreign translations of "Funny Girl" were dropped. The European versions were to be dubbed by the singer to promote the picture internationally as well as representing her own prestigious achievement, but the logistics of learning the entire score in three separate languages proved to be too time-consuming.

When Streisand had first entered the west coast CBS Records' studio to record the soundtrack (separate takes from the film score), she regretted that the familiar microphone from the New York studios was absent, but sound technicians brought it to Hollywood to make her feel more comfortable.

With *Funny Girl* having just been previewed in Milwaukee, CBS Records executives visited the *Hello, Dolly!* location in Garrison, New York to consult the star about the collage of photographs for the album covers, also delivering a million dollar royalty check.

Listening to the soundtrack back in Hollywood, she complained that her breathing had been edited from the takes without her knowledge, the sound later made more natural and spontaneous, especially on the duet with Sharif. Capitol Records re-issued the original stage cast album when the Columbia soundtrack was released, and even before the film opened, more than forty singles and albums of *Funny Girl* material had been recorded by other artists, such as the Supremes and Louis Armstrong.

Columbia Records advertised the soundtrack: "Did you ever think Barbra Streisand would make it big in the movies?" With Streisand and company, the *Funny Girl* soundtrack peaked at #12 on *Billboard*, the two-million-selling extravaganza lingering on the LP lists for over two years, to this day still the longest-charted Streisand album. The soundtrack spotlighted the featured star more so than the Broadway recording, the differences between the two albums being many, chiefly in the deleted songs and their replacements, of course, but also in the richer Hollywood orchestration. With the story "opened out" for the screen, the stage's typically confined and loudish orchestra was replaced by the huge assembly of musicians, including the strings section, able to project the quiet moments when the cinematography reveals intimate close-ups.

Composer Jule Styne considers *Funny Girl* the best film based on his stage musicals but regrets the loss of Fanny Brice's personality in the second half, showing a falsely self-pitying and defeated tragedienne, vulnerable and broken-hearted. He remembers the actual woman as being too strong and too secure and too happy to be distraught for long. The composer preferred the stage original when Fanny resolves not to feel sorry for herself, angrily rejecting her own tears and declaring, "I'll cry a little later, Brice," her resolve hardening. Styne also questioned the modern arrangement of a period number in "My Man," whereas the play's heroine had repeated "Nobody's gonna rain on my parade!"

Barbra Streisand received near universal rave reviews as well as an Oscar and other awards for *Funny Girl*, her film debut marking a career watershed; she never again received unqualified acknowledgment from her peers and critics until *Yentl*, when she was again accorded widespread acclaim. *Funny Girl* reviewers marveled at the bold though well-deliberated innovations in the actress' performance and appreciated the effortless precision with which the musical flowed. Some critics grumbled that the star was too serious in not taking herself seriously, although that deprecation has always been her special strength.

The actress artfully brought freshness and spontaneity into the well-worn lyrics and dialogue, bringing new life to a melodramatic, overcrowded story by brilliantly unearthing the original emotion, going for the real-life inspiration which had been coarsened by lesser talents in mediocre musicals based on the famed Fanny Brice. Streisand was acclaimed for imaginatively re-interpreting the trite formula from *A Star Is Born* as well as depicting an endearing variation upon the theme of a clown whose mask hides deep sadness. Some critics bewailed *Funny Girl*'s not being authentic or that the-unknown-becomes-a-star story was a cliché, although that element of *Funny Girl* at least was true.

The actress-singer's onscreen work was considered more deft and keen than onstage, her comic timing impeccable. Goosebumps were admittedly raised on many a reviewer as well as fan when she ended the musical with the searing Brice standard "My Man." Those who argued against considering the picture merely a Streisand showcase applauded Wyler's subordinating the film's music to the dramatic development.

The *New York Time'* film critic groused that those responsible for the musical had favored their new star so heavily that the production almost overwhelmed her richly-talented performance. Opined Renata Adler, soon to be the paper's ex-film arbiter, "The film has something a little condescending about it-- as though there were some special virtue in making a movie star out of someone who is not likely to be whistled at on Main Street or featured in cold-cream commercials.... Miss Streisand doesn't need any of this." She savaged *Funny Girl* as an "... elaborate, painstaking launching pad, with important talents of Hollywood from the director, William Wyler, on down, treating Barbra Streisand rather fondly, improbably, and even patronizingly as though they were firing off a gilded broccoli."

The critic's disputed contention was that the loving camera gazed too adoringly on the star, although the critic did appreciate the actual Streisand performance, complaining that the film falsified the supposed unattractiveness theme. "She has power, gentleness and intensity that rather knocks all the props and sets and camera angles on their ear." [9-20-68 *New York Times*]

Wyler told reporters how mystified he was about the controversial review, especially considering Adler's unbridled enthusiasm for another film which he considered quite inferior, and the studio officially protested to the editors.

Pauline Kael's *New Yorker* "Bravo!" review applauded the return to the real radiance of yesterday's larger-than-life superstars, but the critic dismissed the cliché that the musical proved that beauty was not a prerequisite to achievement: "The `message' of Barbra Streisand in `Funny Girl' is talent is beauty." Her point about this essential artistic truth was not to reassure the underendowed, not after Streisand rejected the artificial conventions Hollywood had for too long imposed upon the audience with the lookalike, tritely pretty actresses. The woman herself was known to be thrilled by Pauline Kael's comments. In closing this *Funny Girl* chapter, I quote critic Judith Crist's prophetic observation: "She is, in effect, a

startling piece of pop art with a glitteringly evident potential for
permanence.   Revel in her."

# Chapter 22

"An Oscar in April"

Barbra Streisand's *Funny Girl* soundtrack performance received a 1968 best female pop vocalist Grammy nomination, her first in three years, the trophy won by Dionne Warwick for "Do You Know the Way to San Jose?" Elliott Gould projected his wife's Oscar chances with columnist Dorothy Manners: "She works her head off. You don't project as she does without putting out 100 per cent. She may not win an Academy Award-- but I sure do want her nominated. She deserves that." [11-24-68 *L.A. Herald Examiner*]

Dismissing the controversy that he was denied acclaim for directing a significant portion of *Funy Girl*, Herb Ross was grateful for William Wyler's generous and certainly novel credit, "Musical Sequences directed by Herb Ross"-- and Stark requested, in vain, that the Motion Picture Academy designate a special category to preclude shunning Ross, even unavoidably. In February 1969 *Funny Girl* was nominated for an Academy Award not only for best picture (*Hello, Dolly!* the only other such top bid for the actress' films), but Streisand received an acknowledgment for her debut motion picture role, as was widely anticipated. Of the eight nominations, the other honors were: best supporting actress (Kay Medford); best cinematography; best film editing; best sound achievement; best song "Funny Girl"; best scoring for a musical (Walter Scharf).

The advertising campaign to promote *Funny Girl* in the Oscar race was quite extensive, with countless full-page notices in the industry trades from September 1968 through the spring. Columbia and/or Rastar paid for hundreds of ads-- a blitzkrieg never seen since for the actress or her pictures-- but with eight nominations, including a possible top prize, *Funny Girl* was a front-runner, with *Oliver!* the other favorite.

The competition between actresses was unusually ardent, several of the woman having already won Oscars. The odds did not favor Vanessa Redgrave, considered politically controversial, but Joanne Woodward's *Rachel, Rachel* had received the New York Film Critics Award and Patricia Neal's comeback role for *The Subject Was Roses* had followed a serious stroke. The two most likely winners were Katharine Hepburn and Barbra Streisand, even though the legendary actress had won her second Oscar the prior year.

The opposition the youngest actress had to overcome was the vexation veterans felt over the venerable institution's favoring the upstart with early membership. At the beginning of the *Funny Girl* production, Streisand had been selected to join the Motion Picture Academy, a controversial choice defended as the inclusion of an obviously immortal performer. Columnist Sheilah Graham noted that the newcomer benefitted from the bloc voting of three studios-- Columbia, Fox and Paramount-- rival companies investing heavily in their own Streisand blockbusters.

The critical recognition for Streisand's film debut pleased her very much, but she did not expect the Oscar. When a press agent told the actress that a so-far infallible prophet on *The Mike Douglas Show* predicted she would win, she countered, "I'll be his first mistake." Her defense mechanism to avoid the killing suspense of waiting was not to think about winning, bluntly blurting her wish, "I want to win more than anything else in the world, but somehow I can't believe I'm going to get it. It's the Jewishness in me, I guess, the pessimism. It's so close under my skin that old feeling, `I can't win.  Not me.'  It's the agony and ecstasy." [3-5-69 *L.A. Herald Examiner*]

Frank Sinatra and Barbra Streisand were invited to perform on the Academy program expected to be watched by nearly one hundred million, but the actress insisted on lengthy preparations, whereas Sinatra would not rehearse whatsoever the complicated production number, the plan dissipating.  At one time Streisand indicated that her Paris *Funny Girl* premiere companion Maurice Chevalier would escort her to the Oscar ritual, as he had offered.  Gossips speculated that the Goulds' separation announcement preceded the very public Academy Awards to spare the actor the discomfort of escorting his wife to the festivities alike the fabled denouement from *A Star Is Born*.  But she asked him to accompany her, no doubt seeking emotional support through an evening of tension.  It was to be the Goulds' last public outing as husband and wife.

For the first time the Oscar observance which the late Gower Champion produced took place in the lavish new Dorothy Chandler Pavilion of the downtown Los Angeles Music Center, for years the traditional site every spring.  Few gowns worn to the annual Hollywood tradition have incited the controversy as did Streisand's outrageous pantsuit, a clingingly transparent design from Arnold Scaasi.  The "wet and shiny" look appealed to the woman, glassy sequins covering black tulle pants with three layers of shimmering fabric, the top consisting of only two layers, demure white cuffs and collars complementing the outfit.  Streisand elaborated for hours in preparing, undecided between the "pajamas" and a sophisticated Dior gown, finally wearing the costume originally designed for *On a Clear Day You Can See Forever*-- when Daisy's priggish fiancé insists she dress conservatively for a business party, she describes her bold compromise, "It's not too high; it's not too low; it's transparent!"

The controversial, even scandalous Oscar night design had been urged upon the actress.  After the press had ravaged the actress, Arnold Scaasi admitted to fashion arbiter Eugenia Sheppard that he told the star, "Let's show people how young and cute you are. Let's forget that elegant bit." He defended the decision, "Barbra has never been thinner. She is less than a size 8. It's true that my hip-huggers fitted her like a second skin, but they were not tight." [4-21-69 *L.A. Times*]

An opaque body wrap artfully concealed any true nudity. Unfortunately the actress' motives were misread as a defiant affront to the dignity of the hallowed occasion, the revealing clothing forever castigated as a mockery of the august pageantry. Warned that her pantsuit would be audacious, one wonders if the fashion-conscious actress ever regretted the daring attire's ridiculously controversial fallout. Clinging like plastic wrap, the see-all creation shocked society, but just as many people copied her transparent apparel, and today her name is still mentioned every spring as the Oscar anticipation increases.

Streisand disappointed the fans massed behind the celebrity entrance, the actress hurrying into the Pavilion through a side door. She took her seat with Gould, who was seated alongside the late Ruth Gordon, who was married to Streisand's Broadway *Funny Girl* director, Garson Kanin. Another now-deceased film veteran, best actress presenter Ingrid Bergman was visibly shocked when she opened the red foil-lined envelope, the surprise evident in her voice. "The winner is... It's a tie!" The audience gasped. "The winners are Katharine Hepburn in *The Lion in Winter....*"

The sophisticated woman dramatically paused after naming the first of the tie recipients, thus increasing the anticipation. "...and Barbra--" She was unable to finish with the roar from the audience which had applauded the mention of Hepburn but clapped and cheered the second winner.

Hearing that two actresses had tied, Streisand turned an ashen face toward her husband as she grabbed his hand, at that point probably reasonably certain that two actresses of five nominees would include herself. She would recall: "I heard one name, then another. I wasn't sure if it was mine until Elly turned to me and said, `It's you.'" Barbra Streisand and Katharine Hepburn received an identical number of votes from the 3,030 Academy members, the odds of such an acting tie estimated at being 1,250,000 to one. Ingrid Bergman was obviously stunned by the incredible record: "I couldn't believe what I saw!" Surely not a person in the world-- other than the Academy's discreet accounting firm-- would possibly have predicted that the best actress award would be an exact tie. A Price, Waterhouse official had carefully warned Ingrid Bergman to "read everything," but as she told the backstage press, "I thought he was referring to all the names of the nominees."

Seated behind Streisand and representing the other recipient, director Anthony Harvey bent forward to congratulate the winner and proposed that they walk to the stage together. He took her hand, helping her as she stumbled on a platform and tore her suit, when she had to kick the material free from the steps. Her high heel may have caught in the loose bellbottom pants, although the designer would blame a sequin. The crotch seam was clearly visible as she lost her balance, the skimpiest of black panties revealed under the intense lighting. The gossamer material was almost torn from her body, an unprecedented disastrous fall before millions of viewers barely averted.

Harvey accepted the award for the Golden Age actress with a brief speech, during which Streisand reached in gratitude to touch Ingrid Bergman. She clutched her own Oscar in the crook of her elbow to applaud her fellow winner, her pageboy haircut falling modestly across her face when accepting the trophy in her brazen clothing, tears shining in her eyes.

At the second Academy Award, Streisand' speech was flustered and halting but gracious. She began with the quip which was the first line from the film.

Oh-- hello, gorgeous! [Laughter and applause] I'm very honored to be in such magnificent company as Katharine Hepburn. And, uh, gee whiz, it's sort of a wild feeling. Uh, sitting there tonight I was thinking that, uh, the first script of *Funny Girl* was written when I was, ah, only eleven years old. And, ah, thank God it took so long to get it right-- ya know. [Laughter] So, I would, I would like to thank my, my ah, co-producer, Ray Stark, for waiting till I grew up, and, ah, Jule Styne and Bob Merrill for giving me such a great score to sing, and Isobel Lennart for writing such a terrific character, and, uh, and all the Hollywood people who made our show into a movie, ah, Herb Ross, and my dear Harry Stradling, who I haven't let go since, and, ah, my dear friend and director, William Wyler, ah, ah.... It's like, ah [laughs], somebody once said to me-- asked me if I was happy, and I, ah, I said, `Are you kidding? I'd be miserable if I was happy', and I, ah, I'd like to thank all the members of the Academy for, ah, making me really miserable. Thank you.

The joking reference to her "co-producer" was apparently uncaught, the audience not reacting. Having stood aside while the young actress spoke to her assembled peers, Ingrid Bergman took Streisand's hand when they left the podium together. After facing millions around the world, Streisand lost her nerve and delayed fifteen minutes before meeting the press, but the so-called co-holder of the year's Academy Award finally spoke briefly.

Her acceptance speech had alluded to a reporter's interview question about whether or not she was happy. "Maybe some people are basically happy when they're miserable," she explained. "Yeah, it was kind of unexpected, having two winners, huh? I know you won't believe it, but honestly, my work is my reward, and to get this award is just frosting on the cake. But the tension-- I thought I was gonna faint. And I ripped my dress, too. But it was worth it. This Oscar is the essence of awards. And he's naked, too!" A veteran actress tying with a first-timer was natural press material, although Streisand joyfully asked in return, "Who's counting?"

Possibly her surprise was a belief that being a beginner was to be handicapped, that she would win for a subsequent picture-- to this date only three actresses have received debut Oscars, Shirley Booth, Julie Andrews and Streisand, and none since the latter. An Oscar-winning debut has occasionally been considered a jinx for some actors, certainly not true in Streisand's case.

The best actress category was the only Oscar which *Funny Girl* won, but had "People" been eligible as an original song written for the screen, the classic ballad would have been an assured triumph. Nominated for best song, the *Funny Girl* title tune was performed that evening by Aretha Franklin.

Coincidentally, Streisand's friends Marilyn and Alan Bergman won their first Academy Award for writing the best song "Windmills of Your Mind" from *The Thomas Crown Affair*. The best picture winner *Oliver!* was also awarded the best musical score trophy. It seems certain that a split-studio voting crucially hampered the *Funny Girl* totals, too many votes being drained from the picture itself by studio members torn between Columbia's two important musicals.

Winning the coveted Oscar embarrassed the actress because she believed all five performances were exceptionally great, she has recalled. She does not believe art can be divided into five outstanding performances a year, an unrealistically arbitrary nature: one year might contain more than five or none at all.

Nominees and especially winners were expected to attend the exclusive Academy Governor's ball. There the tunic on the winner's beaded pantsuit rose as she was dancing so that photographers shot an even more revealing derrière. Streisand constantly touched and caressed the statuette at the Beverly Hilton festivities. Asked by Dorothy Manners whether sharing the award detracted from her triumph, the actress answered, "No, it just shook me a minute when Ingrid Bergman said `Tie!'"

She predicted, "When I get home I'll pace the floor for hours." Not eating at the ball as friends were waiting for her at home, she nibbled all the cherry tomatoes from everyone's plate at her table. When a photographer shouted a blunt question about why she had worn such an array, she replied to the challenge seriously. "Because I think these are beautiful-- and different." She apologized to her tablemates, "If you'll excuse us, I'll think we'll be running now. Oscar or no Oscar, it's back to work early in the morning." The Goulds left early for Streisand to host her own small party at her rented home, where her officially estranged husband tended bar, but naturally a segment of the Academy population was offended by the early departure.

Katharine Hepburn had raved to columnist Sheilah Graham about Streisand's talent before the award presentation, and the younger actress wired her co-winner, "It's marvelous being in such distinguished company, but do you have to sing, too?" Streisand also thanked the Academy and the entire cast and crew of *Funny Girl* in full-page trade ads. With the controversial clothing, the witty "Hello, gorgeous!" greeting, the unlikely tie vote and the presence of her recently-separated husband as her escort, Streisand was guaranteed to be priority news material.

The day after winning the Academy Award the actress continued to celebrate at *Clear Day* producer Howard Koch's on-the-set party early Tuesday morning. The Paramount producer later recollected the controversial Oscar appearance:

> When Barbra Streisand went on stage to accept the award for `Funny Girl,' everyone thought she was wearing a black pajama outfit that was totally see-through. You could see her rear end. That was all my fault. I was producing `On a Clear Day You Can See Forever' at the time and that afternoon Barbra pulled me into her dressing room and asked me which outfit I liked best on her to wear that night. She gave me a choice of three and I chose the best of them. One was straight and looked awful on her, and the other one was terrible, too. But in those days they had TV cameras that picked you up from behind when you went up the lighted platform to get your award and it looked like she was totally nude. My wife was furious at me for picking an outfit like that. [4-80 *Paramount*]

With many others, paparazzo Frank Teti took pictures of the ecstatic actress at the post-Oscar celebration and observed in his pictorial biography, *Streisand Through the Lens*, "For *Funny Girl*, she was like a little girl who has just won a doll. Her face was totally lit up and she was so excited." He approached her some weeks later when the *Clear Day* actress was on location in Central Park Zoo, showing her the photographs and offering to make copies.

Asking which picture he preferred, she was interested that his favorite was the shot where she looked the happiest. She liked them all, and he was proud to send prints through her representatives.

The Motion Academy voting results are never publicized, but it is suspected that the various contenders usually receive a similar number of votes, with the margin between winning and losing being very close, possibly a differential as scant as only fifty votes or so. Streisand and Hepburn are the only actresses to tie, the only performers ever to have an absolute tie-- once before, Fredric March and Wallace Beery were declared co-winners of the best actor award in 1931-32, but the latter garnered one less vote than his rival. In the early days of the Academy Awards, any three-vote margin constituted a tie, but with the new regulations, Streisand and Hepburn had to receive the same number of votes. It would later be remembered that had Streisand not been a member she could not have voted for herself, that one extra tabulation securing a tie-- it was also noted that it was only fair that she be able to vote for herself.

The Price, Waterhouse accountants are so private about the Oscar outcome that only two executives know the totals, after being counted by eight people who each receive only 15% of the ballots. The winners' names were hidden in a secret safe; tallying the totals is reserved until the very end. One of the two partners involved, Frank Johnson, told a reporter, "Even if someone won by one vote, he would be declared the winner, and no one would ever know it was that close-- not even future generations. The year there was a tie between Katharine Hepburn and Barbra Streisand, I assure you it was a precise tie. We always do at least one recount, but you can imagine all the recounts we did on that one." [3-82 *California*]

Hollywood columnist James Bacon devoted a chapter of one of his books, *Made in Hollywood*, to Streisand. Two weeks after the 1968 Oscar nominations had been released, Bacon received a phone call from a psychic, Dr. Kenny Kingston, who claimed to have been in contact with the real Fanny Brice, who "told" the spiritualist that Streisand would neither win nor lose and that it would be a different musical than *Funny Girl* which would receive best picture honors. Bacon made an oblique reference in his column about the predictions, but he was puzzled because the only other musical contender was *Oliver!*, also from Columbia Pictures. Bacon believed, as was the custom, that each musical would receive much of the studio's votes, thus cancelling each other, *The Lion in Winter* expected to take the prestigious prize. When studio officials called to protest, the columnist tried to explain the good-natured, semi-serious meaning of his writing, and then Stark himself called, lamenting that Bacon had lost the "spiritualist vote" for *Funny Girl*. Whoever Dr. Kenny Kingston is, by pure coincidence or even a true psychic connection-- who knows?-- his prophecies were completely proven valid.

The meaning of the chapter title "Barbra Streisand Owes Me a Lot" was that after an evening of social drinking with a now-deceased friend, Jack Oakie, the film-knowledgeable insider was invited to vote for the Academy member. The columnist was well aware that he himself was ineligible to vote, but the drinking had dulled him. "I voted for Barbra Streisand for best actress. Had I not, Katharine Hepburn would have won the Oscar all alone by one vote." Bacon emphasizes the fact that the actresses won by an exact number of votes. His is an interesting tale, yet any person who voted for Streisand, legitimately or otherwise, could claim the same.

After the Oscar victory, a Lebanese newspaper *Al Moharrer* insisted that films of the "Zionist" Barbra Streisand be boycotted from all Arab theaters "and her film banned," but the threat was empty-handed as *Funny Girl* was still sold out after two months in Beirut theaters. Streisand also received much press coverage in Smyrna, Turkey, where she had pretended to have been born in her first *Playbill* biography during the very early 1960's, and she was soon given honorary citizenship. The newsworthy Oscar tie also influenced fiction works, a point of reference for many authors. Even when *Penthouse* magazine parodied Christina Crawford's *Mommy Dearest* in a satirical story called "Mommy Bitch," the daughter describes her mother Joan Crawford's recovery from the doldrums when Katharine Hepburn won two Oscars in a row for *The Lion in Winter*: "Her resentment eased slightly when she learned Kate had to share the honor with Barbra Streisand for *Funny Girl*."

# INDEX

## Barbra--An Actress Who Sings

## Two great reviews from the *KIRKUS REVIEWS*

## Volume I

The *big* Barbra Streisand book, with not much new, perhaps, but with everything honestly worth remembering pasted together or excellently condensed, and altogether admirable.

Aside from a handful of interviews, Kimbrell seems to have relied on an extensive Streisand bibliography that is much deeper and richer than is usual with celebrity bios, and he's also come up with an inspired method of telling Streisand's story: *backwards*. He starts with her latest failed love affair with TV's Don Johnson (begun when she was 45, he 38)--her latest record, then her live concert at home, then her first songless film *Nuts*, then "The Broadway Album," then the "Emotion" album, then her star-directed *Yentl*, and so on, album by picture by album, as backward reels the mind for decades until, after 400 pages, on april 24, 1942, Barbra Joan Streisand ("so melodic and musical, so lusty and emotional') is born. The advantage here is that the focus is kept strongly on the works, co-actors, producers, and musicians, all of which Kimbrell analyzes with the fascination only a Streisand maniac might muster. No aspect of any work escapes him, from album covers and photographs to Streisand's deep confabs with composers like Stephen Sondheim about the meaning of their lyrics (the recalcitrant "Send in the Clowns"). Kimbrell is clearheaded and candid about Streisand's bad press but is also her greatest defender, meeting head-on her critic's lambastings of her for vanity and egomania and for drowning out any surrounding talents with her own bravura: "this is an artist whose sheer notoriety often precludes appreciation of her vast gift... Antagonists hate not her work but the Streisand *personality*. Even personal adversaries generally acknowledge her talent." He even persuades you she's beautiful.

A very big diamond meant for Barbra's finger.

KIRKUS REVIEWS
2-1-89

# James Kimbrell

**Volume II**

Cool-minded but warmhearted follow-up to the late Kimbrell's first volume of *Barbra* (1989). Kimbrell died of AIDS as that book went to press, and thus this one has been edited by his sister Cheri, who has simplified some of his more literary phrasings and mentions only in passing Streisand's second directorial effort, *The Prince of Tides*, and a new four-CD retrospective album of rare and previously unreleased recording.

Ten years in the writing, the two volumes together have no equal as a midcareer summation of the actress-singer's talents, failings, and successes. Kimbrell has a way of absorbing Streisand's occasional bad press and, without blinking, reversing "egomania" or failure into strength of character and a form of success. In fact, the most outrageous attacks on Streisand, by a foaming John Simon--who time and again is bent on equating narcissism with masturbation-- become laughably vicious as they inventory Streisand's face and character as summits of ugliness. Even the singer's next-to-worst critics herein admit awe of her talent. Volume two opens with slapstick Streisand in *What's Up, Doc?*, Peter Bogdanovich's screwball comedy that Streisand did not want to make, felt uncomfortable filming, and has never liked, despite its being her biggest earner compared to costs. As before, the book moves *backwards*, from 1971 toward the making of her first film, *Funny Girl*, in 1967. Before *Funny Girl* was even released, Streisand had finished the massively mounted (and disappointing) *Hello, Dolly* and was midway through *On a Clear Day You Can See Forever*. Her recording career dipped with the eruption of folk and rock 'n' roll singer-writers, then made a strong comeback as she strove for crossover status from easy-listening nostalgia to hooking into the youth market.

The real goods, a must for fans.

THE KIRKUS REVIEWS
2-1-92

**More great Branden books *by* or *on* Women:**


ACE! Autobiography Fighter Pilot World War Two. Melvyn and Vicki
    Paisley. Highly illustrated autobiography don by a husband and
    wife team, about the more daring flying feats of last great war.
    1943-x $2.95.
ARCHIE MOORE--THE OLE MONGOOSE. Marilyn Douroux. In this
    authorized biography of one of the world's great, Marilyn gives
    more than just the biography of a boxer. Illustrated. 1942-1
    $19.95 c; 1944-8 $39.95 limited edition c.
BARBRA--AN ACTRESS WHO SINGS (BARBRA STREISAND) James
    Kimbrell. A biography of one of the great singers and actresses
    of this century. Illustrated Volume I 1923-5 $19.95 c.; Volume
    II 1946-4 $19.95 c.
BETTER THAN OUR BEST--WOMEN OF VALOR IN AMERICAN
    HISTORY. Ferman/Svihra/Aqualina. Chapters on Hays,
    McCauley, Hancock, Hayes, White, Paul, Adams, Silverman,
    Edwards, Hicks. Ill. 1941-3 $9.95 p.
"BITCH!"--THE AUTOBIOGRAPHY OF LADY LAWFORD. Lady
    Lawford. Lady Lawford, mother of Peter, was witness to the
    vicissitudes of her son and of the many individuals surrounding
    him, including the Kennedys and Marilyn Monroe. Illustrated.
    1995-2 $17.95 c.
CORY--PROFILE OF A PRESIDENT (CORAZON AQUINO). Isabelo
    Crisostomo. A profile of a president. Ill. 1913-8 $19.95 c.
IMPERIAL GINA--THE VERY UNAUTHORIZED BIOGRA PHY OF
    GINA LOLLOBRIGIDA. Luis Canales. Illustrated. 1932-4
    $19.95 c.
A LADY--A PEACEMAKER. Russell Ramsey. First woman president
    of the U.S.A. 1910-3 $17.95 c.
LAST MOUNTAIN--THE LIFE OF ROBERT WOOD. Violet S.
    Flume. Biography of an artist and his techniques--many photos
    and 14 color plates. 1829-8 $25.95 c.; 1878-6 $14.95 p.
LIZZIE BORDEN SOURCEBOOK, THE. Compiled and edited by Da
    vid Kent. It contains actual reference materials and particulars
    surrounding Lizzie's trial. 1950-2 $22.95 c.

MANUFACTURE OF BEAUTY. Ruth Kanin. The *beauty* industry how
it impacts and manipulates standards, making *beauty for profit* a
multi billion dollar business. 1934-0 $12.95 p.

MATTER OF SURVIVAL. Chris Noel. In this autobiography on her
Vietnam War experience, Chris finds herself in direct contrast
with Jane Fonda. Illustrated. 1903-3 $19.95 c.

MISS MARTINE AND OTHER STORIES. Lynn Thorsen. Award-winning short stories. 1928-6 $11.95 p.

MY EUROPEAN HERITAGE. Brigitte Fischer. This is an autobiogra
phy of the daughter of the great German publisher of the Ger-
man-Jewish publisher, Fischer Verlag. Illustrated. 1897-2
$25.95 c.

PARKINSON'S--A PERSONAL STORY OF ACCEPTANCE. Sandi
Gordon. Autobiography of Sandi as a patient suffering from this
dreadful and common disease. Illustrated. 1949-9 $12.95 p.

PRESIDENT'S FAVORITE PLACE (The). Virginia Langley. Visit,
see, discover, write your own Story about President Bush's
Kennebunkport summer residence. Illustrated. 1948-0 $3.95 p.

RED BUTTERFLY--Coping with Lupus. Linda Bell. Autobiography of
a patient battling the deadly Lupus disease. References. 1940-5
$12.95 p.

SARAH PEALE--AMERICA'S FIRST PROFESSIONAL WOMAN
ARTIST. Joan King. Of the great Peale family, Sarah fought
to establish herself as an artist of Franklin, Lafayette, etc. Illustrated. 1999-5 $18.95 c.

SAVING RAIN. Elsie Webber. The Cambodians at the hands of the
Khmer Rouge. 1911-1 $17.95 c.

SINGLE SOLUTIONS--Essential Guide for the Single Career Woman.
Charlotte E. Thompson, M.D. 1933-2 $11.95 p.